EVERYTHING A BABY BOOMER SHOULD KNOW

Before Talking To An Attorney

An Insider's Guide To Estate Planning

EVERYTHING A BABY BOOMER SHOULD KNOW

Before Talking To An Attorney

An Insider's Guide To Estate Planning

by

Mark S. Cornwall

Baby Boomer Publishing
www.babyboomerpublishing.com
P.O. Box 646, Summerland, CA. 93067

EVERYTHING A BABY BOOMER SHOULD KNOW

Before Talking To An Attorney

An Insider's Guide To Estate Planning

by

Mark S. Cornwall

All publishing information or other inquiries should be directed to Baby Boomer Publishing, P.O. Box 646, Summerland, California, 93067. Visit our website at:

EverythingABabyBoomerShouldKnow.com;
BabyBoomerPublishing.com; or
MarkCornwall.com

Dedicated to:

My loving wife D'Arcy,
and the promise that some day,
we too, will have an estate plan.

Personal Welcome

Do the names Jimi Hendrix, Janis Joplin, or Jim Morrison conjure up any memories of excitement and good times? If so, this guidebook is for you. They didn't live long enough to worry about their estate plan, but you did. Congratulations!

Now, what are you going to do about it? Not all estate plans are the same.

One of the reasons people are so reluctant to do estate planning is that it's a depressing subject. It's not much fun thinking about being dead and leaving your loved ones behind. What is worse is thinking about those loved ones fighting over your property and family possessions.

The purpose of this book (along with a couple of other things) is to avoid that scenario. You have worked long and hard and are a generous person. Now you can give one final gift to your family and friends -- an estate plan. It's something like a "Map to the Stars' Homes;" the kind you can buy in Beverly Hills.

An estate plan is nothing less than a map to the stars in your life. It leads to a person, a charity or institution you love, respect or admire. It is also something of a treasure hunt because the object is to get those small or large fortunes from your estate into theirs while paying no tax on the transfer.

This guidebook helps you map out your estate plan so it goes exactly the way you want it to go. It shows you the tools and explains the best ways to give away or preserve your money, homes, businesses, heirlooms, cars, boats, jewelry, tools, art, memorabilia, and every other artifact of life you have accumulated over the last 45 to 65 baby booming years.

The term "estate planning" has its place, like in an old textbook, but it sounds dull and boring. Perhaps the task would be better served if it was named after Hendrix's, *Castles Made of Sand*, or Joplin's *Me and Bobby McGee*, or Morrison's, *The End*. These lyrics more appropriately describe the reasons you need an estate plan now.

TABLE OF CONTENTS

FLOW CHARTS

EVERYTHING A BABY BOOMER SHOULD KNOW

Before Talking To An Attorney

HOW TO USE THIS BABY BOOMER "GUIDEBOOK"

This is called a "guidebook" because it is meant to guide you through the exotic world of estate planning. It is designed to be read from beginning to end as easily as it can be read from the middle to the beginning. The short chapters with topical headings make it easier to jump from one subject to another.

There is no beginning, middle and end to estate planning. It goes on for generations and everything leads to something else you should know. However, it is best to start at the beginning to become familiar with the new lexicon (vocabulary). From there, you can best decide what to do with the information.

The other reason for this shotgun format is that not everyone is interested in the same things. For some, the reading can get technical and make you feel overwhelmed. Those people need to jump to another section that is more passionate about things closer to their heart, such as why you want to avoid a conservatorship, or how to pick a guardian.

But for those that really want to understand what a "three-way formula split with a nonmarital pecuniary formula clause" is, there is sufficient information in this guidebook to give you an understanding – not an education, but an understanding so you will know how to analyze the trust documents and ask questions about how they work.

For others not so keen on reading and understanding every word, you may want to finger through the book to that section explaining how to save your family $920,000 in taxes.

Or for the reader that is married, you need to know what the nonmarital tax exemption is over the next five years in order to plan for its potential affect on your family's inheritance.

There are many, many "terms of art" in this book that every Baby Boomer must know to speak the language of estate planning. In fact, because this guidebook has in it everything a Baby Boomer should know, it is therefore titled to that effect. (Did you know that in the year 2006, there are 7,918 Baby Boomers turning 60 every day?)

In the end you should be able to identify the parts of an average Baby Boomer's estate plan and know how they work. That is one purpose of this guidebook.

Another purpose is to bring awareness to the human side of decision making for estate planning. All the "terms of art" and illustrations of tax exemption techniques cannot help explain your family dynamic. The primary function of estate planning is preserving and distributing your family's legacy. That cannot be accomplished without a serious look at how your family functions, or in some cases, dysfunctions.

This guidebook breaks down the entire system of estate planning so anybody between the ages of 45 and 65 can read it, walk into an attorney's office and, if not tell them exactly what they want, at least be able to discuss the subject intelligently.

It is time for every Baby Boomer, whether you like the moniker or not, to create an estate plan – no more putting it off. You have spent your entire life working; now spend more than a few hours deciding how to distribute your hard earned assets to your loved ones, or your favorite causes.

Author's Disclaimer

This guidebook is not intended to be legal advice or create a lawyer/client relationship. It is for general information and educational purposes only, and specifically to help guide you into an attorney's office.

Every care has been taken to verify that the representations are correct and accurate, but the current state of the law is constantly changing. Do not rely on the legal facts without first checking with a licensed attorney, particularly if you do not live in California.

No opinion herein is a "marketed opinion" and no information provided herein can be used to avoid tax penalties for which the taxpayer would otherwise be responsible. This book provides you with one attorney's perspective of estate planning, and is intended to be helpful in communicating those ideas.

EVERYTHING A BABY BOOMER SHOULD KNOW

Before Talking To An Attorney

AN INSIDER'S GUIDE TO ESTATE PLANNING

First Things First.

From an attorney's point of view there are two ways to approach a potential client's preconceived notion of Estate Planning. Some people believe everything they have heard and read about the Living Trust and think it is either so simple they can do it themselves, or expect it is so common they can buy a one-size-fits-all product at wholesale prices. Those people should look no further.

The best and least expensive forms for estate planning, with thorough explanations on how to use them can be found at:

Nolo's Legal Encyclopedia: Estate Planning
(http://www.nolo.com/encyclopedia/ep_ency.html)

The rest of you will want to use this guidebook to prepare for a consultation with an attorney. This book contains everything you need to know to be a fully informed consumer. The information offered is designed to stimulate ideas on how to protect your family from the legal brouhaha and explore the many ways to distribute your property to your loved ones when the time comes.

The first distinction to understand is the difference between estate planning and financial planning.

Estate Planning uses trusts and wills to build a legal machine (on paper) that controls how you can distribute and protect your assets during your life, and provide a secured legacy for your family after death.

Financial Planning helps you obtain financial goals while you are supporting your desired lifestyle and funding your retirement. A good financial plan builds your legacy.

It is important to understand this difference because financial planners and advisors are selling a product, while the estate planner is selling his services. The author's job as an attorney, for example, is to listen to your goals, determine your needs, and provide the plan to meet those needs; it is not to profit from them.

The goal for any estate planner is to preserve capital and distribute it according to your wishes. You can always go back and adjust your Living Trust or rewrite your Will while you are alive, but after you are gone your estate plan must be strong enough to reach into the future, but flexible enough to change with the times, i.e. family problems or a changing tax code.

Estate planning, in the broadest sense, is the accumulation, conservation, and distribution of wealth in a manner that most efficiently and effectively accomplishes your goals. Obviously it is a goal-oriented activity that uses tax minimization tools to get the most of your wealth to your children, charities, education, special needs, etc.

After reading this guidebook and strategizing with your attorney you will be able to achieve these goals.

What Is Estate Planning *Really* All About? (Peace of mind.)

Once you have determined to whom you want to give your money, the second thing estate planning is all about is not giving your money to the government. Afterall, you already paid taxes on that earned income. You don't want your heirs to pay them again when you die.

7

One way of keeping your estate from going to the government is accomplished by using various "credit shelter trusts." These trusts shift the tax burden so it does not fall on your children after the death of you or your spouse.

The popular trend in Estate Planning is to avoid probate costs and attorney's fees by using a Living Trust, regardless of practicality. A Living Trust (see *What Is A Living Trust*) is not a "tax shelter trust" and is not always the right thing to do. This motivation to avoid "probate" often clouds the fact that for a trust to work you first need someone you can have confidence and faith in, no matter what circumstances may arise when you are gone.

That person who is the object of your confidence and faith is called a "trustee." Much more will be said about trustees later. (See *A Word About Trustees And Guardians.*) But for now, think of the trustee as the one person you chose to carry out your wishes, run your business, look out for your children, sell your properties, manage your investments, provide and protect your family, feed your dog, etc.

If the Trustee is your wife or favorite son or daughter that may be fine, but are they equipped to follow the legal discipline governing a trustee's "fiduciary duty?" Your daughter may be great at making money, but that doesn't prepare her for preserving capital or distributing your funds according to other sibling's needs, particularly if those brothers and sisters are from a "blended family."

Another important aspect of estate planning is to provide a manageable and understandable design of your assets so your chosen trustee can manage your affairs in the event you can no longer do it yourself. Believe it or not, you could become incapacitated due to an accident or incompetent due to health complications.

To be discussed in more detail below is one of the worst tragedies that can divide a family. It is called a "Petition for Conservatorship." This is when a judge decides which of the competing interests, a family member or a professional conservator, will run your family's life from that point forward. (See *Why You Want To Avoid A Conservatorship!*)

Whether it is a Living Trust that funds a "credit shelter trust" after death, or a Last Will and Testament which can do the same, or a combination of both, or none of the above, all it takes to frustrate your plan is a disgruntled heir. Good estate planning includes guarding the plan from malicious interlopers as well as protecting the ones you love. This is why careful thought is so important. Previous planning prevents poor performance!

As an example, consider what would happen if a loved one died in 2006 and left you an estate worth $4,000,000. You could save the sum of

$920,000 in taxes as long as your loved one had taken advantage of a "nonmarital tax deduction trust." (See *The Nuts And Bolts Of The Living Trust.*) Estate planning is *really* about saving your estate for your chosen heirs and making sure it is distributed to them. Nobody else can do it for you.

What Is Probate And What Are Probate Fees?

Many people do not really understand what "probate" is. When we speak of "probate" we are talking about a special legal procedure that takes place at the courthouse, and is governed by the laws in the "Probate Code."

Probate Court does not mean it is a court found in a different location than your local Superior Court. It can be located in the same courtroom where the same judge may also preside over a civil case involving a car accident, or a criminal case involving a murder. Probate Court is in the same place you go to dispute a contract over $25,000.

Probate begins when a "petition" is filed with the court asking the judge's permission to do certain things such as obtain "Letters Testamentary." These Letters allow the executor to gain access to banks and other financial institutions, file tax returns, collect personal property and manage the estate assets, to name just a few.

A "probate referee" who works for the State Government will be assigned to appraise the value of the estate. The referee is paid .1% of the gross appraised value for their services. That value also determines the probate fee for administration as shown in the chart below.

After an inventory and accounting is approved by the court the executor can make the final distribution of the estate assets to the heirs, in accordance with the Will. Of course, any number of legal conflicts can occur between when the Letters Testamentary are issued and final distribution. These conflicts can cause what are called "extraordinary fees" to be paid to the attorney and/or executor.

Below is a chart depicting the Court's filing fee which is determined by the size of the estate.

Size of Estate	Court Filing Fee
Under $250,000	$233.50
$250,000	$305.00
$500,000	$415.00
$750,000	$580.00
$1,000,000	$1,130.00
$1,500,000	$2,230.00
$2,000,000	$2,780.00
$2,500,000	$3,880.00

According to this chart, if an estate is valued at $1.5 million, the Court filing fee will be $2,230.00.

Probate Court is not just for administrating Wills. It has jurisdiction over guardians and conservatorships, trust administration, power of attorneys, health care decisions, and many other issues.

Living Trust Or Will: The Cost Of Probate Is Only Going Up.

The author is a strong proponent of trusts that avoid probate costs and attorney fees. The Living Trust's recent surge in popularity as a way to avoid probate fees has dramatically affected the cost of administrating a Will in Probate Court.

For example, based on an estate valued at $3 million, the present filing fee to administrate the estate would be around $4,000. Considering the median house price in Santa Barbara, California is over $1 million, you can see how many people are affected by the court's intent on making up this lost revenue by increasing probate fees.

State Courts are not going to lose money because of this recent Living Trust phenomenon. As the number of cases filed in Probate Court goes down, the filing fees will very likely go up. And as the fees go up, the number of happy customers goes down. When this course of foreseeable obsolescence finally implodes you can bet California legislators will enact new laws charging a fee for administrating a Living Trust. It will then be necessary to go to another state to avoid Probate. But that long range hypothesis is part of another topic called *Asset Protection*.

For now, you need to decide whether you actually need a Living Trust, or want one only to avoid your preconceived nightmare about probate.

What Is A Living Trust?

A Living Trust is a written document, similar to a set of rules that explains how your estate will be managed. It becomes effective during your lifetime rather than after you die like a Will, and is therefore called a "living" or "inter vivos" trust.

The trust document creates a legal entity such as the "Jones Trust" that can own real property, businesses, cars, and any other asset from which it can distribute assets to you and loved ones both during life and after.

The rules of the trust can be changed during your life, or completely revoked at any time. Therefore it is also a "revocable" trust. It is properly named an "inter vivos revocable trust." Attorneys like to call it a "Revocable Trust" and everybody else calls it a "Living Trust."

It is important to understand that although a Living Trust avoids probate, it does **not** avoid taxes. It can be structured to be a first step to avoiding or deferring taxes. It has no tax advantage over a Will. That is not the purpose of a Living Trust. The types of trusts used to avoid taxes are much more complicated.

As will be introduced in *Planning for the Smaller Estate,* there is no need to avoid taxes if your estate is less than $2.0 million, per person by the year 2006. That means that $4.0 million is already exempt for the married couple, if handled correctly.

Privacy Is An Important Element Of A Living Trust.

The Living Trust avoids Probate, but there is a secondary benefit that may be considered more valuable. Avoiding Probate ensures your PRIVACY. Avoiding probate is like avoiding a long line at the DMV, or at the post office, only everyone gets to look inside your package.

When your estate is in probate court, not only can it be examined by any member of the public that may choose to do so, but it will be scrutinized by court staff, a probate referee, the judge, and perhaps an ombudsman from a governmental agency that feels their duty is to interfere with your family's business.

There are many cases where investigative eyes might be essential to the fair administration of an estate. But if you do not want your affairs open to neighbors, creditors, business associates, long lost relatives and others, then avoiding probate has value beyond the cost of saving money. Better yet, it can help you avoid the process of a conservatorship if you become disabled or incompetent.

Why You Want To Avoid A Conservatorship!

Not enough emphasis can be put on this subject. A very practical way of viewing a Living Trust is as a substitute for a "conservatorship." It is like a cure for an illness because litigation in court for a conservatorship over you is something you want to avoid like the plague.

Not only is a conservatorship proceeding expensive for your estate, but it pits many competing family members, government agencies and financial entities against each other to gain control over your assets. These competing interests range from errant relatives to court appointed "professional" conservators. These professional conservators and their entourage of health care providers and financial assistants can be a disease on your estate.

A Living Trust, on the other hand, can be designed to manage your assets in the event you become disabled or incompetent. In this fashion it works in much the same way as a Durable Power of Attorney, but is more flexible. (To be safe you want both!) The Living Trust can even be designed so that your assets are only transferred into the trust in the event you become disabled. Or if your assets are already in your trust, then only the trustee changes if you become incapacitated.

The one thing you definitely want to avoid is submitting yourself and family to the humiliation of having a conservator assigned to manage your person and your property. This means a stranger manages every minute of your day, and every penny of your money.

Warning! If you become incapacitated and have not directly addressed the issue of who will govern your estate, it will be a starting gun for competitive interests to gain control, particularly where a blended family is involved. This is something to be concerned about. Not only can a wayward daughter or stepchild initiate court proceedings against your wife or husband for a conservatorship, but outside interests, such as banks, security companies, and money management firms may also get involved.

These so-called fiduciaries will contact elder law personnel that can pounce on your estate with a flurry of accusations regarding abuse, regardless of the truth. The next thing you know, a judge will be appointing an unknown professional conservator, at an incredulously high price, to manage your family's every move.

It is not a pretty sight when unwanted strangers move into your house to care for the same person you have been caring for your entire adult life. This can and should be avoided at any cost!

Take It From An Anecdotal Hypothetical #1

As an anecdotal hypothetical, consider what happened to Dr. X and his wife Wilma:

Dr. X was an emergency room physician and had been married to Wilma for 26 years. They both had daughters from a previous marriage, Anna and Beatrice, who had gotten along well during their teenage years before moving out and going their separate ways. Wilma continued to take care of her husband as best as any wife can do.

In his late seventies the Dr. began to exhibit signs of Alzheimer and deteriorated quickly. He could no longer manage his estate and Wilma did the best she could with what little knowledge she had about his financial holdings. She could certainly balance a check book and knew very well the needs of running the house she had lived in for 26 years.

Before long the Dr.'s daughter, Anna, who had very little presence in the home before, began coming by more often and taking items of value from the home. Because she believed, or so she represented, that she was to inherit the house when her father died, Anna somehow finagled personal contacts at the bank to release large sums of money for the remodel of the family home.

About this time Wilma was diagnosed with an early stage of breast cancer and began undergoing treatment, after which she fully recovered. Her daughter from the former marriage, Beatrice, a doctor herself, came home from Arizona to help take care of her mother and Dr. X, her step-father. This is when all hell broke loose.

Anna began a full verbal attack on Wilma for not being able to properly care for her father, and accused Beatrice of imposing on the family home and leaching off her mother (thereby leaching off Anna's potential inheritance). Even though Anna, as the Dr.'s daughter, is not the favored relative by law to be appointed as her father's conservator, she nevertheless petitioned the court for the appointment so she could gain control over his estate.

Ironically, the first person by law to be considered the best conservator for the Dr., or any other incapacitated husband, is his wife; which in this case was Wilma.

Unfortunately for Wilma, Anna's vicious personal attacks and unfounded lies about Wilma's incompetence and Beatrice's hidden agenda to leach off the estate were heard by the court. Anna sought alliance from her friends at the bank and got it, if only to protect the bank.

Based on that information the Judge decided to:

- Assign a court appointed attorney to represent the incompetent Dr. X;

- Order a professional conservator to be appointed by the court attorney;

- Order health care providers to live in the family home 24 hours a day;

- Order every penny that Wilma spent to be authorized by a bank trustee;

- Order Beatrice and Anna restrained from the family home; and

- Order strict visiting hours for Beatrice and Anna to visit their mother and father.

In this hypothetical it should come as no surprise that the court appointed attorney, the conservator, the health care provider service and the bank trustee are all friends, and all will extract large fees from Dr. X's estate. This was not the first estate they were appointed to and it won't be the last. That is the way the "conservatorship system" operates.

If proper precautions are not taken in your Living Trust then the next estate to get pillaged by the system may be your own. Then, and in that hypothetical case, every last shred of dignity will be stripped away by people you don't even know.

So the moral of the story is: get a Living Trust.

For a startling review of the subject, look up the excellent journalistic expose of the private world of conservators and guardians that ran in the *Los Angeles Times* beginning Nov. 13, 2005. The articles investigate the unsupervised world of court-ordered professional caregivers and reveal the ramped abuse of the elderly these "professionals" are ordered to protect. The series began in Sunday's edition of Nov. 13, 2005 and is available for free on-line at your local library.

Does A Living Trust Save Money By Doing Your Chores?

As discussed, a Living Trust can help avoid huge potential problems, but for most people it does not necessarily save money. Think of it like this: when your spouse or parent dies, there is a lot of work to be done by somebody. This is when you hope the trust has been properly funded and all affairs are in order, or you will end up in Probate Court anyway.

There is the funeral, the paperwork to access bank accounts, the safe deposit box (how do you get in?) the location of stocks, bonds, insurance policies, IRAs, retirement and pension funds, the management of these accounts, the paying of bills, conclusion of personal matters, selling of businesses and other real property, dealing with partners, and filing personal income tax, inheritance tax and perhaps federal estate tax returns.

Then there is the process of accounting for personal property and dividing it among heirs, and perhaps the family residence that may have to be vacated and sold.

These chores cannot be avoided. Leaving it all for an attorney to do would be expensive. But with the help of a Trustee, one that is disentangled from family politics and not subject to unrealistic demands and bias, can be the only person to get the job done right. Once again, choosing the right trustee is an integral part of managing a successful distribution of an estate.

What About A Will And Attorney Fees For The Small Estate?

Whether the decedent (the person who died) has a Will or not, if the entire value of their estate, including real and personal property, does not exceed $100,000, and the heir to the estate is readily identifiable, then the property can be collected and distributed without the need of probate administration. (The value of the estate excludes joint tenancies, IRAs, insurance policies, etc.)

The heir or beneficiary can obtain their interest in personal property by using an affidavit or declaration alone. In order to accomplish the transfer of real property the heir or beneficiary must file a declaration and petition to the court requesting the estate's real property be conveyed to them. Does that sound easy? If so, just follow the instructions beginning at Division 8 of the Probate Code.

The Probate Code also offers a family protection plan for the small estate whereby the surviving spouse and minor children can petition the court to have the family homestead "set aside" in order to protect it from creditors.

If the net value of the decedent's entire estate does not exceed $20,000 (over and above all liens and encumbrances including the probate homestead) then a petition may be filed to have the estate "set aside." This, in effect, is permission from a judge to be excused from probate (Probate Code § 6600).

Therefore, if your estate, or that to which you are entitled to by right of succession, is less than $100,000, present your paperwork to your local attorney and have him/her draw up the papers "setting aside" the estate for a nominal fee.

Attorney's Fees

For all those Wills that are not excused from probate, much ado is made about the cost of paying attorney fees. These fees are regulated by statute and there is little argument that a huge estate valued at millions of dollars will carry a huge attorney fee based on a percentage of the estate's value.

But little is ever said about the personal representative, called the "Executor," who receives exactly the same compensation for his services as the attorney. Any executor has a right to waive this fee for the benefit of the other heirs to the estate, but this author has never met one.

In fact, the personal representative normally hires the attorney, but essentially becomes the attorney's helper. It is anticipated the executor is familiar with the estate and will act as liaison between family business and legal business.

In order for you to determine if you feel these fees are extraordinary, the scale for compensation in California, based on the appraised value of the estate, is as follows:

1. 4% on the first $100,000;
2. 3% on the next $100,000;
3. 2% on the next $800,000;
4. 1% on the next $9,000,000;
5. ½% on the next $15,000,000;
6. For estates above $25,000,000 a reasonable fee will be determined by the court.

Estate Value	Statutory Fee
$100,000	$4,000
$200,000	$7,000
$300,000	$9,000
$400,000	$11,000
$500,000	$13,000
$600,000	$15,000
$700,000	$17,000
$800,000	$19,000
$900,000	$21,000
$1,000,000	$23,000
$2,000,000	$33,000

Based on this scale, the compensation paid to the attorney and the executor on a $1.5 million dollar estate is $28,000.00 each, for a total of $56,000.00.

Are The Statutory Attorney And Executor's Fees Worth It?

The answer depends on if you believe administration of your estate may need supervision.

When you consider the average estate for the moderately successful Baby Boomer in California is approximately two million dollars, you begin to wonder if these fees are worth it. Afterall, once you are gone there is nothing more an attorney or executor can do to save the estate money beyond what has already been planned.

On the other hand, if you do not use the services of probate, nobody is supervising whether the job is done right. Unless there is a trustworthy person in control of the money, and savvy in business and personal affairs, there are a lot of well intentioned mistakes that can be made.

Personalities can clash, greed can raise its ugly head, and power can corrupt. Choosing the players in your estate becomes a matter of checks and balances on your priorities. Only you know what is best for your family.

PLANNING FOR THE SMALLER ESTATE

Preliminary Thoughts On Planning For The Smaller Estate.

The first question in Estate Planning is whether or not your estate will be subject to estate taxes upon your death. This is determined by examining your age and annual income, your present assets with growth potential, and your expectation of inheritance, etc.

In the years 2006, '07, and '08, the estate tax begins at $2,000,000. This means that if your estate is valued at $2,000,000 or less, and you die in 2006, your estate will pay no Federal taxes. But if your estate is worth $2,500,000 and you die in 2006, it will be taxed on the overage of $500,000. If you die three years later, in 2009, this exemption amount changes to $3,000,000, and your estate would be taxed on any amount over $3,000,000. (See *How the Federal Tax Exemption Works.*)

Assuming your estate is under $2,000,000 in 2006 and thus exempt from taxes, it may be possible to plan its administration using either a Will or a Living Trust. Planning for this smaller estate is relatively simple and probate cost and attorney fees can be easily avoided when a client's desires are straight forward.

The tools for Estate Planning become more creative when the scenario changes to blended families with children young and old, ex-spouses and/or premature deaths, contested community property, business partnerships, hazy ownerships and other individual considerations.

Once the assets are identified it must be determined how to distribute them. For example, is it better to hold ownership of real property with your daughter in joint tenancy with right of survivorship, or should a Totten Trust be implemented which gives her a right of survivorship, but no rights until death? Or instead of money to the children upon death, should a Family Pot Trust be created so as not to distribute the entire sum of money until the youngest child reaches a certain age? And if you have a disabled child, perhaps a *Special Needs Trust* is appropriate.

There are many important decisions a husband and wife must make. What happens when the first spouse dies? Where will his or her separate property go? How will the step-up in estate value affect the surviving spouse? Will a Bypass (non marital, tax shelter) Trust be necessary? What happens if a spouse remarries? What about a guardian? Who will be trustee?

Although these options are overwhelming at first, particularly in light of impending mortality, you can rest assured that a well planned estate is the best gift you can leave your heirs. Estate

Planning is not an unnecessary expense; it is a positive and virtuous legacy used to avoid chaos after a lifetime of work. With sound legal advice and knowledgeable tactics you can provide yourself and loved ones a great feeling of security.

There is a popular Trust package being sold these days at various seminars that promise all you need, regardless of your individual estate, is a Living Trust – kind of a cookie cutter claim that one size fits all. *Caveat Emptor!* A Living Trust, standing alone, only works for the smallest estates with someone trustworthy enough to administrate it in your absence.

Avoiding probate cost should not be your only goal, particularly at the expense of your loved ones. Providing a thoughtful and secure system for distributing your wealth after you are gone is the goal. Your Estate Plan is your last chance to speak.

HUMAN CONSIDERATIONS AND THE FAMILY DYNAMIC

A Word About Trustees And Guardians.

One of the shortcomings of a Will is that when both parents are gone the assets of the estate are generally given outright to the children if they are eighteen or older. Some of them may not be ready to manage this windfall profit and would greatly benefit from a trust.

There are many trusts and trustees to choose from to help guide children until a certain age. A trust for the children's benefit can be very flexible, or not, depending on the desired goal. Would it be only for their education? Would it be distributed at ages twenty, twenty-six and thirty? Could they buy a car at age eighteen? What exactly would it mean to provide funds for their needs?

These are all good questions that can be answered with the appropriate directive in the trust. A directive is an actual statement explaining your intentions. But what every Trust needs in order to work is a good Trustee.

The value of a good Trustee cannot be overstated. A Trustee has the highest fiduciary duty prescribed by law, meaning he or she must act with well intentioned reason and sound judgment regarding your affairs at all times.

The Trustee is given serious responsibility to look after the best interest of people ranging from minor children to disabled grandparents. This is often in exchange for very little payment, even though they are managing potentially hundreds of thousands of dollars in the trustee's trust.

They are expected above all else to preserve the capital of the trust account, while at the same time tempering that duty by maintaining the lifestyle of the beneficiaries. This means the trustee must not only be a prudent investor, but a compassionate friend to those they serve. It is not an easy job and demands a constant balancing act in order to make people happy.

Therefore, you must decide who is right for the job. It is not the same as choosing a guardian for your children. A guardian is chosen because of their loving nature, their shared moral integrity, their ability and willingness to accept your child or children into their house, their financial wherewithal to provide for additional children, the size of their house, the town, the school, and their ambient family nature, etc.

Would you allow a stranger to choose a babysitter for your kids? You may name a guardian in your Will or Trust which the Judge will consider seriously when he appoints a guardian. If there are competing parties, the judge will decide who will be guardian according to what he perceives as the best interest of the child.

A Trustee should be a person familiar with your business that preferably knows you, and will use this knowledge to make the best decisions for you in the future.

If you do not know a person you can trust in that role, than an attorney whose life and career experience has been conducted as a model of fiduciary duty, may merit consideration. Ethically, however, it is not normally regarded to be in the family's best interest to have the attorney who writes the trust also serve as the trustee.

Banks Or Professional Trustees?

When you choose a trustee you need to take the above mentioned qualities into consideration. Banks often have departments that specialize in managing trust accounts, and professional trustees are well-suited to accept substantial deposits and distribute money by computer. However, that says little for their human qualities.

These institutions normally view trust funds as though the money was bequeathed to them. They are simply not equipped to handle the day-to-day needs of a person with any compassion. They generally are not equipped to personally service the "smaller" beneficiary.

A Few More Important Words About A Trustee

Before you pick a trustee, or request someone to act as trustee, think of what you are asking of them. You are putting them in a position of serious responsibility and perhaps a target for unruly or dissatisfied heirs.

Not only must they manage the "money" you accumulated over your life, but either "may" or "shall" distribute the principle of the trust to beneficiaries. This means they either "shall" distribute the trust funds based on reasonable proof of the beneficiary's needs, putting the beneficiary more in control; or "may" distribute the funds, leaving distribution of the funds up to the trustee's sole discretionary power.

These issues of who controls the distribution of trust funds, and by what standard of discretion the trustee may use to distribute those funds, are governed by the language used in the trust. That is why standard "boilerplate" forms are tricky if you don't know what you are doing.

In the case of "shall" distribute the funds, the beneficiary is more in control. If the beneficiary does not get the funds they have requested from the trustee, they can sue the trustee and win if they can persuade the judge they have a reasonable need (for plastic surgery?). This is because the trustee is under a direct order to release funds in such a situation.

On the other hand, if the trustee "may" distribute the funds, the beneficiary has little control because even if they can show they have a reasonable need, the trustee is under no order to distribute funds to them. Therefore the judge is less inclined to order the trustee to pay the beneficiary, regardless of their perceived "reasonable need."

It does not take an attorney to see the potential conflict brewing between the trustee and the beneficiary when different priorities collide. The only instructions left to the trustee may be language in the trust telling them to provide for the beneficiary's "health, support, maintenance and education," or "comfort, welfare and happiness." What does that mean to the trustee trying to preserve the principal? What does it mean to the beneficiary that wants to take a trip abroad?

Remember that whatever your relationship with the Trustee, whether he or she is a trusted friend, a professional, or a bank, it ends upon your death. The Trustee is left to figure out if providing for your daughter's health includes plastic surgery, or if providing maintenance and support includes buying tools for a mechanic's garage, or art for an art gallery, or instruments for a medical lab.

For every dollar spent on Johnny's musical training at Julliard, there is a dollar taken from Suzie's need for world wide travel. That creates friction and makes the trustee a mark for litigation. The accusations will be breach of fiduciary duty and abuse or bad faith.

One of the most important principles of the family dynamic is that your presence and relationship with the family members may be the very magic that ensures everybody gets along. Without you, your family is left to their own resolve. This can produce some pretty selfish results.

Some Ethical Considerations, e.g. Who Does Your Attorney Represent?

The estate planning should begin before you meet with an attorney. Upon making an appointment you should be sent a *questionnaire* such as the one that can be found in the Appendix of this guidebook.

The questionnaire in this Appendix is designed for *married persons,* but is easily adaptable for a single person. (A single person's estate is simpler because of no ownership issues). You are required to fill out these forms to the best of your ability. This mental exercise will prepare you for the breadth and scope of estate planning. Even if you only read it, you will better understand the task at hand.

If you are married you must determine if the attorney will represent both of you, or just one. If you have been married to the same person and share the same children, then the answer may be easy.

But what if:

- Each party wants confidential advice and guidance concerning their separate property;

- It is a recent marriage and one spouse has substantially more than the other;

- Both parties have substantial separate property and need separate planning;

- Each party desires to pass their separate property to different persons;

- One party has corporate holdings that have been in his or her family for years;

- The attorney also represents business partners in a family business;

- One spouse wants to take unfair advantage of the other;

- Outside interests are competing to gain favor over each spouse;

- The attorney represents the bank or trust company?

In these situations it may be necessary for the attorney to have frank discussions with both parties concerning the desires of the other spouse. This may not be desired by either party.

Therefore bringing another attorney into the planning may be prudent regardless of the fact it cost twice as much. However, experience has shown most people, regardless of wealth, are unwilling to bear that cost no matter how smart it is.

Leaving It All To The New Wife

One thing any experienced estate planner will attest to is the common phenomena of the man whose wife dies after thirty years of marriage. Let's call them Bob and Joan. Bob then remarries a younger woman in due course. The children of the first marriage are grown and moved out of the house, or perhaps to another state.

In a majority of cases, if there is no plan in place at the time that Joan dies, Bob will scrap any notion of leaving both their property to the adult children, and will inevitably leave it all to the new wife. It happens all the time. The children, he feels, are old enough to take care of themselves and his loyalty is to the woman with him at the end.

You can be certain this was not Bob and Joan's intent while they were married and in their discussions before she died. But this situation can be avoided with proper estate planning.

This is accomplished by implementing an irrevocable trust that is automatically created at the time of the first spouse's (Joan's) death. This would have prevented the initial plan from changing. Bob could have received the benefit of all Joan's separate community property during the course of his life, but upon his death, Joan's property in the trust would be distributed to their children.

Of course, alternatively, Bob could draw up a Will leaving his entire estate to his adult children when he died, but that would be difficult to do in the face of his new wife.

"Spousal Fiduciary Duty" Husbands and Wives *Must* Communicate – Truthfully

What a concept! This is something the law has developed to help balance any business acumen or financial advantage one spouse may have over the other. It helps regulate their confidential relationship regarding community property transactions between themselves. For example, suppose Husband wants to leave the family residence to a daughter of a previous marriage, including Wife's community share.

The Husband's fiduciary duty to Wife, and vice versa, is the same as that between business partners. He must explain what he wants to do and put his plan in order without putting Wife's estate at an unfair disadvantage. If Wife is okay with giving up her share of the residence, than she must put it in writing. Otherwise the gift would be voidable.

There is a duty (Calif. Family Code § 721) between husband and wife to give true and accurate information regarding anything that affects their community property transaction. It imposes a duty of the "highest good faith."

This means that if there is any Agreement between spouses that the court deems unfair to one, the Agreement is presumed to be a breach of their spousal duty and can be undone through legal action.

Leaving It To The Children.

As for leaving money to children, there is much to take into consideration depending on the age and temperament of the child. (See *A Word About Trustees.*) The older you get the more outrageous it seems to leave a large sum of money to an eighteen year old.

It is commonly recommended that a trust be used to stagger payments between the ages of 23, 26, and 30. The expectation here is that at

23 your son will want to buy a Porsche, at 26 he will have graduated college, and at 30 he will have settled down and know what he wants. For others, the ages of 20, 30 and 40 sound more appropriate.

Yet some parents may want to provide for their children's education and then leave the rest of the money to charity. This is easily accomplished through a wonderful tax saving device known as a "charitable remainder unitrust."

This trust known as a CRUT is very flexible and will allow you to, among other things, sell stocks with a very low tax basis at a very high price, and not pay any taxes on the stocks or highly appreciated real estate. Whether used to pay for the education of your daughter, or provide a percentage of the income to you for retirement, a CRUT is a valuable tool in estate planning. (See *Charitable Remainder Unitrust.*)

The normal prerequisite of a trust for children is that it protects the *corpus* (that amount of money in the trust) from them; thus the name "Spendthrift Trusts."

Another way of helping a young adult manage their money rather than keeping it from them, or forcing it on them, is to allow them to withdraw money from the trust as they believe they need it. This essentially allows them to be their own trustee without the responsibility of managing the entire sum of money in the trust.

One way to manage children's money is to establish a Family Pot Trust that can be distributed to each child in accordance to their needs, according to the trustee's discretion or by the terms in the trust. Another way is a Minor's Trust; another is a Custodial Account, etc.

Ergo, there are many ways to plan your child's inheritance. Most parents are afraid that a trust may be a distraction for a young person. They believe it might rob them of their incentive to go out in the world and do well. More than one child has been lured away from college, or taken up a life of drugs because the easy money was there.

These concerns can be relieved by language in the trust that stops money when the child is not enrolled in college full time, or fails to maintain a certain grade point average, or gets arrested more than once, or violates some other standard of conduct in the trust.

THE BLENDED FAMILY (The Blended Extended Family)

The "Blended Family" Now Includes 60% Of Americans.

It is estimated that 60% of the population lives in a blended family. The term "blended family" is a modern term of art. It defines that family where the parents are on their second or third marriage and have both step children and perhaps common children of their own.

The step children may live in the same house, but most likely are adults with a large disparity in age with the new children. They have little in common with these younger children because ten or twenty years have passed since that first or second marriage ended – which means there is a wife # 1, and/or a husband #2, etc. Think of Mike and Carol of the Brady Bunch divorcing and remarrying a third partner.

In the dictionary the word "blended" is defined as "to mix smoothly and inseparably together." Given that definition and the character of the typical "blended family," the term should probably be changed to "unblended family."

Dynamics such as age differences between children of prior marriages and the new children, may breed animosity. Petty jealousies can arise. There was less money in the estate when the older children were young and perhaps the new spouse brought wealth to the marriage to which the prior children mistakenly believe they have a right.

Now they are young adults and their own wealth status and desires are not similar to the needs of the new minor children. And of course, the adult children's loyalty is to their own mother.

From a litigator's point of view, this family is living in a volatile world and subject to "probable litigation" upon the death of the first spouse. This can happen when the estate has something to fight over, or in some cases, anything to fight over whatsoever.

What To Do About The Blended Family Dynamic?

The best way to understand what to do in the blended family situation is to understand what will happen if you do nothing. Remember that all of us have an estate plan whether we like it or not.

The government of California, as with every state, has devised a plan that will distribute your assets upon your death in accordance with the rules found in the Probate Code.

All you have to do for these rules to apply to you is to die without a Will or some other non-probate estate plan. This is called to die "intestate." This means that the beneficiaries of the estate will be identified by statute and fixed by the court rather than by the deceased mother or father. (See *What if You Die Without A Will Or Living Trust?*)

The legislative policy for "intestate succession" (to whom your property goes) reflects a paternal instinct in the law to protect and provide for the surviving spouse and minor children. This policy is designed for the "traditional family."

There are even laws to protect the welfare of the decedent's surviving family to the exclusion of named beneficiaries in a Will, or against creditors, if it appears they will exhaust the estate of individuals in the family that are protected by law, i.e. surviving wife and child.

This is all fine and good for the traditional family of hard working Bruce, and stay at home mom Kathy Jones, who have been happily married for twenty-five years, and have two healthy boys whom they love dearly. If Bruce dies, the estate will go to Kathy and after she dies to the two children equally. No problem.

But what about the older Tom and younger Cindy Smith? Tom is 60 years old and Cindy is 40. Tom has two adult sons from a previous

44

marriage of twenty-five years, and two grandchildren. Cindy and Tom have been married five years and have a daughter three years old.

If Tom dies without a Will or Trust his adult children will be surprised to find that Cindy is in control of everything, and entitled to most of their father's estate. This is regardless of how much separate property their father took into the marriage with him.

The new wife will end up with all the community property and as much as two-thirds (2/3) of Tom's separate property. This happens as follows:

According to the laws of intestate succession, Cindy is entitled to all community property; including Tom's half of the community. That part you may have suspected. But as Tom's wife at the time of his death she is also entitled to one-third (1/3) of his separate property, regardless of where it came from or how large its value.

In addition, Tom's three year old daughter is also entitled to one-third (1/3) of the remaining two-thirds (2/3) of Tom's separate property, which she will share equally with his two sons. But because the daughter is a minor, her share will pass directly to Cindy. Therefore, Cindy is entitled to all of the community property and almost two-thirds (2/3) of Tom's separate property.

As you can see, these default laws greatly benefit the surviving spouse and/or child of the "traditional family." In the case of Tom and Cindy Smith the laws give no consideration to Tom's grandchildren, and little thought to the sons of his previous marriage.

What's more, Cindy is entitled to take an administrative fee as Tom's executor which is equal to the fee of the attorney she hires, and she also inherits the "power of appointment" over the estate. This means she determines who the heirs of Tom's separate property will be as long as she leaves a Will or Living Trust.

In other words, Cindy is not holding the property in a life estate which passes to Tom's children or grandchildren when she dies. It is all Cindy's, and in all fairness it cannot be thought of as Tom's anymore since he gave it away, albeit unintentionally.

Unfortunately, this can be a difficult pill for Tom's prior children to swallow. Had his wishes been otherwise, Tom could have drawn up a simple estate plan that distributed his life's earnings more evenly.

What If You Die Without A Will Or Living Trust? ("Intestate Succession")

Dying without a Will is not necessarily a bad thing. But as shown above, the California laws governing the distribution of a person's estate that does not have a Will or Living Trust (called the laws of intestate succession) heavily favor the surviving spouse or child, to the exclusion of a child from a previous marriage.

As you read the chart below to see how intestate succession works, think of an example where there is a bachelor with no children from a previous marriage and whose parents have predeceased him.

Suppose this lonely bachelor left a Will leaving his entire $2 million estate to the California Hemp Society. When the bachelor's very poor brother and sister find his Will while rummaging through his house after death, what might they be tempted to do with the Will? Now there is a question for Angela Lansbury!

California's Intestate Succession Chart For Married And Unmarried Decedent	
If you are survived by a:	**Distribution (after court costs, creditors, lawyers, and specific gifts)**
Spouse and child; or more than one child	Surviving spouse is entitled to all the community property and half of decedent's separate property. The other half of the separate property goes to their child at age 18; if more than one child the surviving spouse takes 1/3 of the separate property and 2/3 is shared by the children equally. (If child has died their share goes to their son or daughter)
Spouse, and a child by previous marriage.	Same as above. The surviving spouse takes all community and half the separate property, and other half of separate property goes to child of previous marriage. If more than one child, spouse takes 1/3 and children share 2/3 of separate property equally.
Spouse and a parent or parents, but no child	If the decedent has no living child, and no grandchildren, then spouse takes all community and half the separate property, and the other half goes to decedent's parent, if only one is alive. If both are alive they take 2/3 of separate property.
Spouse and no child, grand child or parent, but sister and half brother	When all lineal descendants are deceased then half of separate property goes to spouse and other half is shared between half and full brothers and sisters, equally.
Child only; or Spouse only	If surviving child only, the child takes all. If surviving Spouse only, spouse takes all.
Not married and no children	All to parents or surviving children of parents (brothers and sisters and/or their surviving issue) if parents are not alive.
None of the above	All to grandparents or surviving children of grandparents (cousins and surviving children of deceased cousins)
No relatives	State of California

How You Might Be An Heir To Millions Of Dollars.

Although the above scenarios apply to most situations, there is still a way that you could inherit millions of dollars from that rich tycoon you never heard of before:

Suppose the tycoon was married once in his youth, but his wife predeceased him and he died an unmarried man with no children.

Then assume the tycoon's parents had predeceased him and he had no brothers and sisters. Assume further that his grandparents are also dead and there is no living aunt or uncle or cousins that are descendents of those grandparents.

Now assume that the former predeceased wife's parents, from long ago, are no longer alive and there are no other descendents of those parents such as a brother-in-law or sister-in-law to the tycoon, or their children that are still alive.

Now assume that the tycoon has no next of kin of any kind that can be found, and that you are the nearest relative, such as a third cousin by marriage, of the predeceased wife! .....and *Voila!* You are the lucky heir to the millionaire tycoon's legacy.

THE NUTS AND BOLTS OF THE TYPICAL LIVING TRUST

The "Typical Living Trust"

Below is a diagram of a stereotypical Living Trust where the husband dies first between the years 2006-2008 when the marital tax deduction is $2,000,000 per spouse.

This typical family received some notoriety back in the '60s when their Pa, Ben Cartwright, settled down with his three sons: Adam, Hoss and Little Joe, on the Ponderosa Ranch near Silverado. Each son had a different Ma from a previous marriage, but Ben finally struck a Bonanza when he married Kitty, fresh off the stage from Tombstone.

What's right for Ben and Kitty may not be right for you. Some of the estate planning decisions Ben Cartwright makes may be considered foolish by some, while others would consider them generous. But for educational purposes, the following should help point out why one estate plan does not fit all.

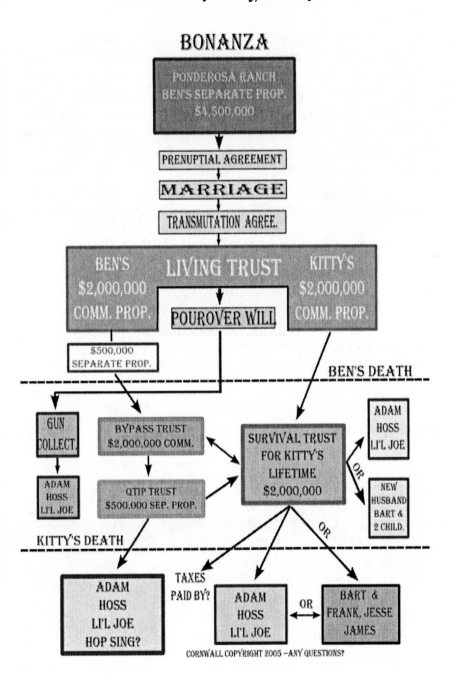

BONANZA

PONDEROSA RANCH
BEN'S SEPARATE PROP.
$4,500,000

PRENUPTIAL AGREEMENT

MARRIAGE

TRANSMUTATION AGREE.

BEN'S $2,000,000 COMM. PROP.   LIVING TRUST   KITTY'S $2,000,000 COMM. PROP.

POUROVER WILL

$500,000 SEPARATE PROP.

BEN'S DEATH

GUN COLLECT.

BYPASS TRUST $2,000,000 COMM.

SURVIVAL TRUST FOR KITTY'S LIFETIME $2,000,000

ADAM HOSS LI'L JOE

ADAM HOSS LI'L JOE

QTIP TRUST $500,000 SEP. PROP.

OR

NEW HUSBAND BART & 2 CHILD.

OR

KITTY'S DEATH

ADAM HOSS LI'L JOE HOP SING?

TAXES PAID BY?

ADAM HOSS LI'L JOE

OR

BART & FRANK, JESSE JAMES

CORNWALL COPYRIGHT 2005 -- ANY QUESTIONS?

This chart is a little beyond the scope of our discussion because it includes prenuptial and transmutation agreements which will be covered under *When Death and Divorce Collide.* But if you follow how the boxes flow together you can understand how it can serve as a prototype, and can be retooled for anybody's estate.

As you examine this flow chart and begin to understand what Ben and Kitty have planned for themselves, the following questions begin to arise:

- Wouldn't Ben want to leave money to his sons outright upon his death?

- Aren't the boys too old to wait for their inheritance until after Kitty dies?

- Couldn't Ben somehow secure the Ponderosa for his sons?

- Why would Ben give so much of his separate property to Kitty?

- Can't Kitty be stopped from giving her part of the estate to her new husband?

- Did Kitty actually remarry and sire two boys named Frank and Jesse James?

- What about Hop Sing?

These are the types of questions that for many come too late. The purpose of understanding estate planning is to ask the questions beforehand while there is still time to do something about it; or make certain that the plan delivers exactly the desired outcome.

Here are some oversimplified definitions of the typical living trust tools used by Ben and Kitty:

Living Trust (Revisited)

As stated above (see *What Is A Living Trust*) a Living Trust is a written document like a Will, but it becomes effective during your life time rather than after you die. It is therefore called a "living" trust. The trust is a legal entity that can own real property, businesses, cars, and any other property or cash from which it can distribute funds to beneficiaries.

As stated previously, the proper name of a Living Trust can be tricky because it is identified by other names for different reasons. Because the "rules" of the trust can be changed any time during your life, or completely revoked, it is sometimes called a "revocable trust." The proper legal terminology for the trust is an "inter vivos revocable trust." Many attorneys refer to it as a "Revocable Trust," but most people call it a "Living Trust."

There are three good reasons to use a Living Trust instead of a Will.

1. It avoids probate.
2. It allows for easy management of assets.
3. It is the perfect segue into the Survivor, Bypass, and QTIP trust, as described below.

A Living Trust provides the same function as a Will in that it distributes property to your heirs upon death. But in addition to avoiding the cost of probate administration, there are other headaches a Living Trust helps you avoid.

The trustee of the Living Trust can act more quickly to administer and distribute the estate without being bogged down by court supervision. With a Will, the executor can do nothing but hire a lawyer without court permission.

But to get that permission the attorney must file a petition to administrate the Will, then a petition to confirm sales of property, petitions for instructions, petitions for almost final distribution, then one for final distribution, and on and on it goes until typically a California probate can last at least one to two years. A typical trust can be administrated in months.

Furthermore, in addition to helping avoid the cost and trauma of a conservatorship proceeding during Husband or Wife's lifetime, the

Living Trust provides long-term continuity of management of their estate without being interrupted by their death or incapacity. (See *Why You Want To Avoid A Conservatorship!*)

It must be remembered, there is no Living Trust without a husband and wife transferring legal title of the assets into the trust. This demands time and expense to re-title the property and transfer it into the name of the Living Trust. Ben and Kitty Cartwright would have to re-title ownership of the Ponderosa to Ben and Kitty, Trustees of the "Ben and Kitty Living Trust."

Likewise, they must do the same with all the farm equipment and animals, and even their arsenal of weaponry. This could be accomplished with a "Bill of Sale" identifying all equipment and stock and guns to be delivered into the Living Trust.

Pourover Will

Every Living Trust needs to have a Pourover Will. A Pourover Will not only reiterates the last testament of the decedent, but works to "pour" assets into the Living Trust if they had not been transferred to the trust prior to the death.

This would be the case if Ben Cartwright failed to transfer ownership of his gun collection into the trust before he died. The Pourover Will allows the gun collection to pour into the trust (after probate if its value is over $100,000) so it can be distributed to Adam, Hoss and Little Joe in accordance with the provisions of the Living Trust.

The same goes for the ownership of newly acquired property, such as Ben's last acquisition known as the "South Forty." If it was never transferred into the Living Trust by Ben, then his executor of the Pourover Will, his oldest son Adam, would do the job upon Ben's death. The property could then be distributed to Kitty and/or the three boys in accordance with the Living Trust; perhaps placed in the Bypass Trust or the QTIP Trust.

The downside is that if the "South Forty" and/or the gun collection property have a value over $100,000, then a probate will be necessary to transfer the assets into the trust. This is another good reason to update your Living Trust every so often.

Survivor's Trust

Once the Living Trust comes to an end upon Ben's death (remember this is a stereotypical example) it automatically divides into two separate trusts. In our simplified example Ben has died first and his half of the $4,000,000 of community property in the Bonanza estate is going into the Bypass Trust discussed below.

The other half of the estate, because Ben has "transmuted" (See *Transmutation Agreements Can Save Big Money; Or Not*) most of his separate property into community property, goes into Kitty's Survivor's Trust.

Acting as her own trustee, Kitty has complete control over the property in the Survivor's Trust and the trust property avoids probate just like in a Living Trust. The Survivor's Trust is administered for the sole benefit of Kitty, by Kitty, and she is entitled to every bit of the monetary distribution of its principal and income for life. She can choose to share the income of this trust with the three boys, or not.

The Survivor's Trust is also revocable at any time meaning she can do whatever she wants with it. And because she also retains the "power of appointment" over the trust property she can leave whatever is left in the trust after she is gone to whomever she wants. It doesn't have to go to Adam, Hoss, or Little Joe, as is the case in the Bypass and QTIP trusts discussed below.

Also, in this scenario of a $4,000,000 community estate (excluding Ben's separate property) there will be no tax payable upon the death of either spouse because neither of their trust will be more than the $2,000,000 Federal tax exemption allowed.

Bypass Trust

The Bypass Trust is also known as the "exemption trust" or the "B trust" or the "family trust" or the "credit shelter trust" or the "nonmarital trust," as well as other names. Do not let this lead to confusion because there is no need for it.

All of these names refer to the same trust used to save money from Federal estate taxes by properly utilizing the "applicable exemption amount" of the nonmarital tax exemption, which in this case is $2,000,000. (See *How The Federal Exemption Tax Works.*)

If any spouse puts their $2,000,000 share of the estate (called a "nonmarital tax deduction") into a Bypass Trust for the surviving spouse's benefit during their lifetime, the surviving spouse will not be taxed on that $2,000,000 at 46% if she dies in the year 2006 ('07, '08).

What is left of the $2,000,000 in the Bypass Trust (called the "remainder") when the second spouse dies will go to the spouses' children, or some other heir that both the husband and wife agreed upon when they entered into their Living Trust.

For example, in the Cartwright's estate plan the "Bypass Trust" is used as a standard planning tool to make Ben's half of the community property assets available for Kitty's use for her lifetime.

But none of the remaining assets in the Bypass Trust will be added to the gross value of Kitty's estate when she dies.

This saves tens of thousands of dollars in estate taxes as you know from reading *How The Federal Exemption Tax Works* and studying the chart. Ben's Bypass Trust will "bypass" Kitty's estate and be handled separately, unlike the QTIP Trust.

Assuming Ben and Kitty each have a $2 million interest in the $4 million portion of the Bonanza estate, Kitty's half can save $920,000 in taxes by not including Ben's half if she dies in 2006. If Ben does *not* put his share into the Bypass Trust, his $2,000,000 will be added to Kitty's $2,000,000 and her estate will be taxed on that $2,000,000 at a rate of 46% upon her death. That's a $920,000 tax bill to Kitty's heirs, whether they are Adam, Hoss, Little Joe, Hop Sing, or Jesse and Frank James.

On the other hand, Ben's $2,000,000 in the Bypass Trust is not only tax exempt from Kitty's estate, but even if it appreciates in value over the years, all of the appreciation will not be taxed as income to the three sons. There is no estate tax on the increased value of the Bypass Trust.

Kitty can be the trustee of the Bypass Trust and may even be able to invade the corpus of the trust if she can show a "reasonable need" for her "health, support, education, and maintenance."

However, if any of the appreciated assets are sold while she is alive, she or the three sons will have to pay a capital gains tax on the appreciated income.

But this is where you can see trouble brewing. Whether or not a trip to Europe would be a reasonable need for Kitty is the big question. The Bypass Trust becomes irrevocable upon the death of Ben, and Kitty has no power to change the beneficiaries named in the trust document. Therefore Adam, Hoss, or Little Joe could bring a lawsuit against Kitty to stop her from invading the trust corpus and wasting the assets to pay for her traveling expenses.

Not allowing Kitty to change the beneficiaries in the Bypass Trust keeps the money from going into the hands of the wrong people, in the mind of the deceased Ben. But he has no control over how much of the trust will actually be left when Kitty dies. He has no control over Kitty's spending. (But a separate trustee, other than Kitty or the boys, would have control over the spending, and might be a good idea.)

Some spouses are justifiably concerned about their spouse's spending habits and therefore a QTIP trust may be an appropriate alternative to the Bypass, or a thoughtful addition if the estate is large enough.

QTIP (Qualified-Terminable-Interest-Property) Trust

The QTIP Trust can be as complicated as the acronym implies but is widely used as an estate planning tool. There are specific requirements that must be met based on the Internal Revenue Code. For example, all of the income from the trust must go to the surviving spouse for life and there can be no authority to change that.

It is the only form of "marital deduction" that gives Husband control over the disposition of the trust property after Wife dies by distributing it to his specified beneficiaries. The property interest is "terminable" because it ends upon Wife's death.

As a "marital deduction" any amount of money can be added to the QTIP Trust from Husband's estate tax free. But upon Wife's death the remainder of the QTIP Trust is added back into Wife's estate and will be taxed if it is over her $2,000,000 tax exemption.

Thus in Kitty's case the $500,000 remainder in the QTIP Trust will be added back into her gross estate when she dies and be taxed at 46% on all amounts over the "applicable exclusion amount" which in 2006 is $2,000,000. (This language is technical but it is the language that will be used in the estate documents.)

For example, if Ben Cartwright's share of the Bonanza estate was $2,000,000 in community property and $500,000 in separate property he may want to put the $2,000,000 in the Bypass Trust for Kitty's health, support, education and maintenance, and to save Kitty's estate $920,000 upon her death; *and* put $500,000 in a QTIP Trust so that sum could pass directly to his three sons upon Kitty's death.

Kitty will receive an annual income from the QTIP Trust generated from the $500,000, but she is not allowed to invade the core assets of the trust for any reason. (These core assets are also referred to as the corpus, assets, principal, funds, property, money, remainder, etc.) Upon her death, the "remainder" of the trust avoids probate. It is also free from Kitty's creditors, and automatically passes to Adam, Hoss, and Little Joe with no further fanfare.

Kitty's heirs to her Survivor's Trust pick up the tax bill on the amount over $2,000,000 in the QTIP. Therefore, bottom line is that the QTIP Trust only defers taxes on the $500,000 from Ben's estate. But if Kitty's Survivor's Trust has dwindled in value down to 1.5 million before the QTIP is added back into it after her death, then there would be no taxes to pay on her estate.

By using the QTIP Trust, Ben has assured himself that his sons will receive at least $500,000 of his estate regardless of how Kitty's spending habits might otherwise affect it.

Ben's primary concern may secretly have been that recognizing that Kitty is still a young and attractive woman that she may remarry and not feel compelled to leave as much of the Bonanza to Adam, Hoss, and Little Joe as Ben would have liked. The QTIP becomes irrevocable upon Ben's death and cannot be changed.

Special Needs Trust (SNT): A Special Consideration

When there is a child, friend or family member with a disability that allows them to receive government aid, a Special Needs Trust (SNT) can set aside property for that person in order to supplement their aid without making them ineligible to receive government assistance.

Most government aid programs require the recipient to have resources and income below a certain level, such as SSI, Medi-Cal, IHSS, subsidy housing (section 8), etc. In other words, the programs providing aid to people with no financial resource larger than $2,000.00. (However, that does not mean you can't set up a SNT for someone less fortunate.)

For example, when a disabled person receives an inheritance gift or personal injury award of substantial value they have three choices: 1) they can go off assistance, 2) spend it all until they are poor again, or 3) get a SNT.

The SNT allows the trustee to fund money for the purchase of certain items which are not counted by the government as "financial resources." This would include a home of any value, a vehicle of any value, household goods, and other social and medical services available to the disabled person.

Preparing the Special Needs Trust requires the attorney to be familiar with the specific requirements of the government programs for which the beneficiary may be eligible, and that can be difficult in the midst of constantly changing law.

Nevertheless, the SNT can be the perfect tool for the right situation and should be considered if you have money and a disabled parent, child or friend.

What To Do With This Nuts And Bolts Information.

With the information you have just read, go back and stare at the Ben and Kitty Cartwright flow chart. Look at all the boxes and follow the arrows to their destination, and/or their alternative destination.

If you take the time to do so it begins to become clear how the tools of estate planning can work for you. This is a prototype for every estate plan, including the very large estates.

To help visually stimulate your understanding there follows two bonus "BONANZA" flow charts. The first one applies to Kitty and the boys if she continues to live the "traditional" lifestyle; and the second chart applies to a lifestyle where she remarries and goes her separate way.

BONANZA -- TRADITIONAL

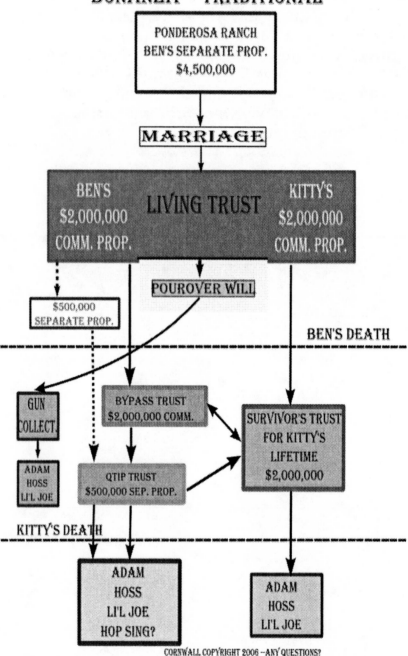

PONDEROSA RANCH
BEN'S SEPARATE PROP.
$4,500,000

MARRIAGE

BEN'S
$2,000,000
COMM. PROP.

LIVING TRUST

KITTY'S
$2,000,000
COMM. PROP.

POUROVER WILL

$500,000
SEPARATE PROP.

BEN'S DEATH

GUN
COLLECT.

BYPASS TRUST
$2,000,000 COMM.

SURVIVOR'S TRUST
FOR KITTY'S
LIFETIME
$2,000,000

ADAM
HOSS
LI'L JOE

QTIP TRUST
$500,000 SEP. PROP.

KITTY'S DEATH

ADAM
HOSS
LI'L JOE
HOP SING?

ADAM
HOSS
LI'L JOE

CORNWALL COPYRIGHT 2006 --ANY QUESTIONS?

66

BONANZA -- REMARRIED

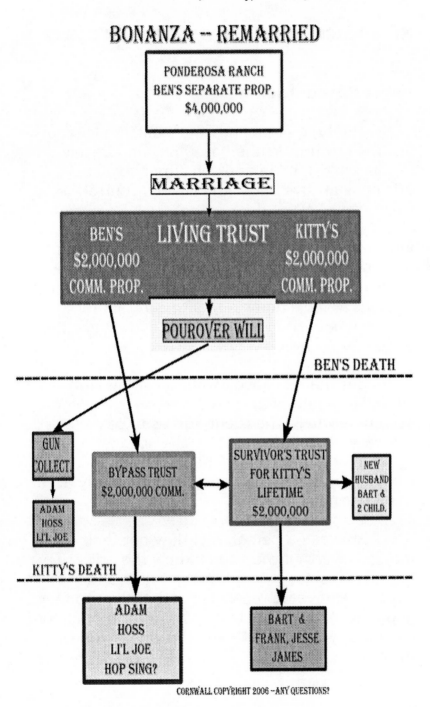

PONDEROSA RANCH
BEN'S SEPARATE PROP.
$4,000,000

MARRIAGE

BEN'S
$2,000,000
COMM. PROP.

LIVING TRUST

KITTY'S
$2,000,000
COMM. PROP.

POUROVER WILL

BEN'S DEATH

GUN COLLECT.

ADAM
HOSS
LI'L JOE

BYPASS TRUST
$2,000,000 COMM.

SURVIVOR'S TRUST
FOR KITTY'S
LIFETIME
$2,000,000

NEW
HUSBAND
BART &
2 CHILD.

KITTY'S DEATH

ADAM
HOSS
LI'L JOE
HOP SING?

BART &
FRANK, JESSE
JAMES

CORNWALL COPYRIGHT 2006 --ANY QUESTIONS?

67

HOW MUCH DOES AN ESTATE PLAN COST?

Value Based Pricing

The type of pricing you should be looking for in a law firm is one based on "unparalleled product satisfaction and consumer service." Pricing is always under the client's control.

The author's law firm operates on an innovative system called "value based pricing." The customer only pays for what they want by knowing well in advance the price they are willing to pay. No consumer wants to contract for professional services when they don't know the price.

But that is exactly what most law firms expect of a potential client. The typical billing system is where the client agrees to pay the attorney for the hours he or she spends performing a particular job; then waits in great trepidation to see the damage, particularly at $500 per hour.

How can a person feel they got their money's worth if they don't know the price they are going to pay? In addition, the price has to be equal to the value received for the client to feel good. Nobody wants to pay a Corvette price for a Mustang, yet they both get you where you want to go.

In estate planning with a value based firm, you are able to build your own vehicle. If you want high performance down to the last QTIP, there is a price for that. If you want it straight and to the point, there is a price for that too.

The fact of the matter is that everyone's needs are different. But regardless of needs, the attorneys using value based pricing can be assured their price is based on the most "efficacious" services.

"Efficacious" in this context means a price based on the lawyer's "ability to accomplish a job with the minimum expenditure of time and effort." This is what is known as "value" in the world of legal services.

It is not based on the size of your estate or the overhead of the attorney. You do not make up for the under-billed time spent on another client. The fee is based solely on what you are willing to pay.

If you later decide you want the attorney to work beyond the scope of your work order, you may place a "change order." This way the client is always in control of the price.

Below are four fee examples. The actual price is established at the first consultation. These four examples are not "boilerplate" forms where your name fills in the blank.

Each one is a legal tapestry woven by your needs as determined from your answers to interview questions. Some are simple and others are elaborate and take a great deal of time to complete.

All combinations are unique because of the professional service that accompanies them. Here are some typical billings for 2006.

Single person, $1,295.00 receives:
> One Living Trust
> One "Pour-Over" Will
> One Advance Health Care Directive
> One Durable Power of Attorney for
>> Property Management
> One Trust Transfer Deed
> Notary Services
> Unlimited assistance

Married couple, $1,995 receives:
> One Living Trust
> Pour-Over" Wills
> Two Advance Health Care Directives
> Two Durable Powers of Attorney for Proper
>> Management
> Certification of Trust
> One Trust Transfer Deeds
> Notary Services
> Unlimited assistance

Married w/children, $2,495 receives:

       One Living Trust

       Two "Pour-Over" Wills

       One Guardianship Directive

       Two Advance Health Care Directives

       Two Durable Powers of Attorney for
           Property Management

       Marital Property Agreement

       Tangible Personal Property
           Memorandum

       Certification of Trust

       Two Trust Transfer Deeds

       Trust Funding Assistance

       Notary Services

       Unlimited Assistance

Married w/children, children from previous marriage, and other beneficiaries, $3,495 receives:

       One Living Trust, including:

       One Survivor Trust

       One Bypass Trust

       One QTIP Trust (if needed)

       Two "Pour-Over" Wills

       One Guardianship Directive

       Two Advance Health Care Directives

       Two Durable Powers of Attorney

       Marital Property Agreement

       Tangible Personal Property memo

       Certification of Trust

       Trust Transfer Deeds

       Trust Funding Assistance

       Notary Services

       Unlimited Assistance

There are many reasons why none of the above combinations are right for you. It depends on your personal, family and financial needs.

WHY YOUR ESTATE PLAN MUST BE REVIEWED

As the Greek philosopher Heraclites claimed as an axiom of eternal truth, "The only thing that remains the same is constant change." Because the times are still changing so should your estate plan when certain events occur.

Your plan needs to be reviewed and updated on a periodic basis, such as every three or four years as the children advance from high school to college to marriage, to divorce, etc.

For example, it is malpractice for an attorney not to advise his client in writing that they should update and revise their will after their divorce has been finalized, or even before.

Other routine changes that trigger an automatic review of your Living Trust or Will are marriages and/or separation after marriage; a new birth or death in the family, a change in your job or financial fortune, inheritance from your parents, a change in your health condition, changes in the tax law, etc.

Consider one of the most routine facts of life that strike 50% of American families. Assume your son or daughter, whom you love dearly, has chosen to marry the wrong individual. It may seem obvious to you that your child's divorce is imminent if they don't change their ways, but it may take years for them to figure that out.

Unfortunately, your Will or Trust leaves the full value of your estate to your child at age 30 and he or she is now turning 28. It seemed like a good idea ten years ago to leave that money to him/her at such a mature age, but now you know the money would only be squandered on nothing productive. This is when you review your Trust or Will and change the final distribution date to your child at age of, say, 40.

Some people don't even realize this power is available to them. They think once the decision has been made and the documents signed it has been cast in iron. This is not so. Another common example of reason for change is news of a terminable illness for the spouse that was expected to outlive the survivor. This happens all the time and changes have to be made to save on taxes.

Lastly, given the fact the entire Federal estate tax plan is going to be repealed one way or another in the year 2010 means that your estate plan may have to be modified and should be reviewed. But it is not a good reason to wait until after 2010 to create an estate plan.

Whatever your case may be, you need to proceed to *Planning for the Larger Estate* to get a better idea of the additional tools available to satisfy your potential needs in the future.

PLANNING FOR THE LARGER ESTATE

It is a common misconception that Estate Planning is only for the wealthy, but after reading the foregoing seven chapters of reasons why every Baby Boomer needs to plan their estate, that common misconception should now be dispelled.

Estate planning is, of course, essential for those who have accumulated substantial wealth, but it is also important for those of modest or moderate wealth as well. Every dollar lost unnecessarily to taxes or administrative costs hurts the survivors more when the estate is small.

What Is A Larger Estate?

There are three factors that decide whether you need to plan for the larger estate:

1. The size of your family;

2. How much money you want to save them; and

3. The aggregate value of your assets.

The primary purpose for married couples to utilize Trusts, after the avoidance of probate, is to preserve assets for long term beneficiaries, and to avoid tax losses upon the death of the surviving spouse.

As an alternative, you can leave all of your estate to your surviving spouse and not a single penny of a billion dollars will be paid to taxes at the time of your death. This is called the Marital Deduction. If your spouse dies in 2006, for example, the entire value of the estate over $2,000,000 will be taxed at a rate up to 46%.

How The Federal Exemption Tax Works

First, you have to be married. Second, your spouse has to be a U.S. citizen. Third, each spouse has an opportunity during their lifetime (not after death) to set aside from their share of the estate the "Federal Tax exclusion limit" which in the years '06,'07, and '08 is $2,000,000. This is $2,000,000 that the family does not have to pay estate tax on when the first parent dies.

This "applicable exclusion amount" will also never be included as part of the surviving parent's estate, so the children will not be taxed on the money at the death of the second parent either. This is not the case with the QTIP trust. (See *The Nuts And Bolts Of A Living Trust.*)

This means you can put $2,000,000 (your half of a $4,000,000 estate) into a credit shelter trust, such as the Bypass Trust, when you die and this money can sit tax free to be used for the benefit of your surviving spouse during their entire life.

Then, the $2,000,000, or what is left of it, will pass directly to your children upon the death of the second parent. The children do not pay federal tax on either the $2,000,000 that was in the Bypass Trust, or the $2,000,000 left by the surviving spouse.

It should be noted again that there is also a "marital tax deduction," which is the alternative to the tax exemption. This deduction allows a Husband (or Wife), as stated above, to leave their spouse any amount of money they want, even $1 billion upon their death, and the surviving spouse will not have to pay any tax on it. They could use the entire amount to support any kind of extravagant lifestyle they preferred.

However, if they died in 2006, any amount of that $1 billion that is left over in the estate when the surviving spouse dies will be taxed at 46% on all portions over the $2,000,000 exemption. That is exactly why a Bypass trust is so beneficial. It allows a larger amount of your estate's value to go "tax free."

The chart below shows how legislators gradually raised this tax exempt amount for each spouse's estate beginning in 2001: from $675,000 in 2001 to $2,000,000 in 2006.

The column at the right shows the highest tax bracket for each year at which an estate may be taxed on all sums above the exempt amount, and unlimited in 2010. In 2001 it was 55% on amounts over $675,000, and in 2006 any amount over $2,000,000 may be taxed up to 46%, etc.

YEAR	AMOUNT EXEMPT FROM ESTATE TAX	HIGHEST TAX BRACKET
2001	$675,000	55%
2002	$1,000,000	50%
2003	$1,000,000	49%
2004	$1,500,000	48%
2005	$1,500,000	47%
2006	$2,000,000	46%
2007	$2,000,000	45%
2008	$2,000,000	45%
2009	$3,500,000	45%
2010	Unlimited	N/A
2011	Must wait to see what legislators enact.	

Again, each spouse has the opportunity to set aside the "nonmarital tax exempt amount" of their estate value before they die. In 2006, a husband can put $2,000,000 into a trust from his estate for the benefit of his wife, and ultimately for his children, without them having to pay a penny of tax when their Mom dies. (Of course, that is only fair since the earned income has already been taxed by the government! But it may also include highly appreciated assets.)

More importantly, if the husband fails to exclude this amount from his estate by setting it aside in trust, he forfeits the right to exclude the applicable amount and it will be taxed after the death of his surviving wife. If she dies in 2006, '07, '08, the heirs will have to pay $920,000 in taxes on $2,000,000.

Also, keep in mind that the estate tax, above, and the federal gift tax, (see a comparison with *Generation-skipping Tax,* below*),* are unified tax exemptions, not "in addition to" exemptions.

In 2002 the gift tax exemption was raised to $1,000,000. The estate tax and gift tax are mutually exclusive in that they draw from the same exemption pot.

Therefore: If you give $1,000,000 in gifts (in addition to the annual exemption that was raised to $12,000 in 2006) it is subtracted from the estate tax exemption when you die. ($2,000,000 in 2006 − $1,000,000 gift tax exemption = $1,000,000 estate tax exemption.)

The Capital Gains Tax May Replace The Estate Tax.

If you are wondering who is responsible for this generous change in tax laws, it was President George W. Bush. But before you give him a big pat on the back, consider that if Congress does nothing before the year 2010, it is anticipated by many professionals that the capital gains tax will replace the estate tax. This means that the $200,000 mortgage on your $2,000,000 house will "carryover" to the heirs of your house.

As it stands now, the house's value is reappraised at death and its cost basis is "stepped up" to $2,000,000 (fair market value) for the heirs. If your son or daughter sells the house they pay no income tax.

But in 2011 the house will not "step up" in value at death and your son or daughter inherits the $200,000 cost basis. If they sell the house they pay taxes on $1,800,000.

The Titanic Of All Estate Planning: The Legacy of Rupert Murdoch

Here is the Titanic of all Estate Planning:

Mr. Murdoch is the 73 year old media mogul with an estate valued at around $35 billion. He owns such companies as the Fox Network, and the New York Post, along with another 186 publications he owns in a company called the "News Corporation."

He has billions of dollars in assets strewn throughout the world – particularly in Australia, New Zealand, Britain and America. He also is a former owner of the LA Dodgers baseball team, as local baseball fans will remember.

Mr. Murdoch's blended family includes four adult children, and two infant children. These six children include his daughter Prudence, by his first marriage; Elizabeth, Lachlan and James, by his second marriage which ended in 1999; and Grace 3, and Chloe 2, by his present marriage in 2005.

Mr. Murdoch has recently announced that all of his children will be treated equally in the distribution of his estate, but rumor has it that the heir apparent, his eldest son Lachlan, age 33, has quit the family business because of this sweeping change in his father's inheritance plan.

The new plan allegedly makes the third wife, Wendi Deng, the most powerful player in the family trust because she will act as guardian for her two infant daughters until they can claim their inheritance at age 30. That's three votes for Wendi, and only one vote for each of the adult children.

This new property distribution plan also invalidates the previous deal Murdoch struck with his second wife, Anna, during their divorce proceedings in 1999. That deal granted Anna's children, along with Prudence of the first marriage, control of the trust in the event of Murdoch's death. The new deal substantially reduces the power of Mr. Murdoch's four adult children to...well, less than they want.

It would be nice to think that with $35 billion dollars in trust all of the beneficiaries could be happy, but who knows? If the dynamics of this blended family spiral out of control and into the "exploding turkey scenario" (which may not be applicable to this Australian family) there will be enough legal work here to keep a thousand attorneys fighting into the next millennium. And you thought your situation was diverse, volatile, or downright complicated!

Bringing Big Concepts To Big Challenges

People in the league with Mr. Murdoch already have buildings full of attorneys. However, Estate Planning is not like business law because it requires substantially different skills. It requires attorneys who have affirmative people skills, not adversarial skills, and the ability to listen and work personally with the client.

It is not the intent of this guidebook to provide sufficient legal knowledge to write your own estate plan. You would have to go to law school and practice law for twenty years in order to do that right. It can get quite complicated and demand the use of several professionals to work in coordination. The information provided here is intended to stimulate ideas so you can better understand your needs and communicate them to your attorney.

As your estate grows larger, the more need there is for using the various tools allowed by the Internal Revenue Code in order to sculpt your estate into a work of legal art. But every estate is different. Consider the different family needs that must be served between Mr. Dentist and Mr. Plumbing Contractor (pseudonyms for real live people).

Different Strokes For Different Folks

1. Dr. Dentist is 55 years old and still married to his first wife, Nora. They have two minor daughters in private school and live in a 10,000 square foot home on an exclusive golf course. They buy a new car any time they want. Both the girls are equestrian riders and Nora is busy managing their home, the kids and charity events.

The Dr. has a twin engine Golden Eagle airplane he uses to commute to his other lucrative dental practice in another town. Besides their residence, they own a cabin in Lake Tahoe and a large medical office in downtown Santa Barbara which he purchased with two other partners. Dr.

Dentist has received good financial advice over the years and developed a well rounded securities portfolio worth over $2,000,000.

Besides his own IRA and 401K for the office, he has set aside money for his daughters' educational fund. Dr. Dentist also provides for his mother who lives nearby and is in her eighties.

DR. DENTIST AND NORA

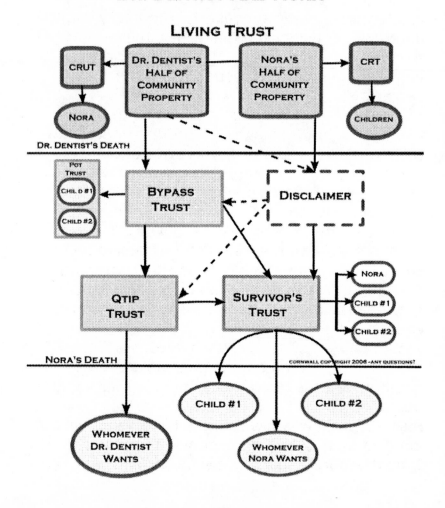

LIVING TRUST

CRUT

DR. DENTIST'S HALF OF COMMUNITY PROPERTY

NORA'S HALF OF COMMUNITY PROPERTY

CRT

NORA

CHILDREN

DR. DENTIST'S DEATH

POT TRUST

CHILD #1

CHILD #2

BYPASS TRUST

DISCLAIMER

NORA

CHILD #1

CHILD #2

QTIP TRUST

SURVIVOR'S TRUST

NORA'S DEATH

CORNWALL COPYRIGHT 2006 –ANY QUESTIONS?

CHILD #1

CHILD #2

WHOMEVER DR. DENTIST WANTS

WHOMEVER NORA WANTS

2. Walt the plumbing contractor is 55 years old and has been working in the plumbing business for thirty-five years. He has recently married his third wife. He has two previous wives with whom he shares four adult children, but has always been the only parent with the financial means to help them.

The first two children from the first wife are in their thirties and each of them has two children, giving Walt four grandchildren. Walt's second two children from the second wife have just reached college age. His oldest son, Derek, helps manage the plumbing business.

Walt has been successful as a plumbing contractor, but also earned windfall profits from investments in California's ever increasing real estate market. The appreciation in his residence alone over the last ten years has netted him $1,200,000 in equity.

There is also a condo he purchased up the coast in 1990 for $125,000, which is now worth $425,000. He owns an old office building he bought downtown in '92 for $475,000 and after redevelopment it is now worth 2.2 million dollars. Along with a couple of other rental houses he owns and rents, his "net" value in real estate is $3.5 million.

The appraised value used by the probate court is the "gross" value of his properties, which, if he died today, would be $5.5 million. On top of this is the appraised value of the plumbing business and equipment.

Which Of These Two Scenarios Is Most Challenging?

Neither, they are juxtaposed with the same level of individual complexity but little in common after that.

The Dr. and Walt's primary needs go in opposite directions. Dr. Dentist's primary need is to provide for his wife and the future of his minor children (referred to above as the "traditional family"), and for his mother should something happen to him first.

Walt has recently remarried after toiling 35 years to build his estate. His "primary" need may be to provide for his adult children and his grandchildren, while assuring security for his new wife. Walt's situation is something of a balancing act.

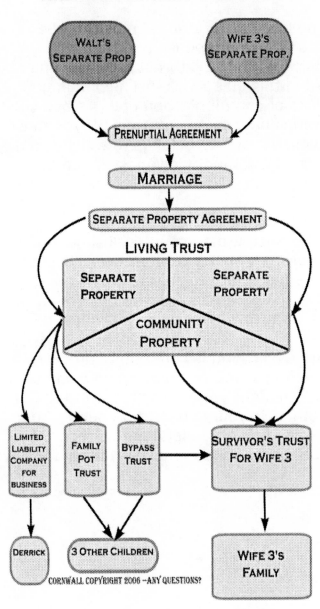

WALT THE PLUMBING CONTRACTOR

CORNWALL COPYRIGHT 2006 –ANY QUESTIONS?

Priorities And Property "Characterization" Must Be Discussed

The issue of "priorities" must first be discussed with your spouse and then communicated to the attorney. Questionnaires provided in this guidebook are helpful in getting those lines of communication open. Once your beneficiaries have been determined, you must decide which property belongs to which spouse, and which is community or quasi community property.

These are not always easy subjects to discuss because it may sound selfish identifying your separate property as your own. But it is absolutely necessary to characterize your property as separate in order to determine who can give what to whom, as an individual gift.

Not everything is community property! That inheritance you received years back, or that house you bought earlier, or that painting from your brother, is your separate property. Your attorney can be very helpful in this regard by offering a dispassionate analysis of the goods you own.

Some of the other questions couples need to discuss are:

1. Will you need separate representation? (See *Who Does The Attorney Represent?*)

2. Is there a premarital agreement to consider?

3. What are your tax objectives?

4. How will, or can, life insurance affect your estate?

5. Who will be trustee – spouse, friend, professional? (See *A Word About Trustees.*)

6. Should a surviving spouse be sole trustee for the credit shelter trust?

7. Who will be guardian of your children? And who will handle their funds?

8. Who gets the "family heirlooms?"

9. Are there clear lines between your spouse and previous children?

10. Are you speaking truthfully about exactly what you expect?

Once this type of dialogue is under way, you can begin connecting the dots between your priorities with legal tools that are designed to do just that.

In addition to the trusts tools discussed in *The Nuts And Bolts of The Living Trust*, the larger estates may want to utilize more specialized tools such as a "three-way formula split with marital deduction pecuniary formula clause," and a "disclaimer trust" as well as a "reverse QTIP trust," and definitely a "Sprinkling Trust," (also called a "family pot trust") for the children with distribution in three stages, and a Trust for children of a previous marriage in two stages, and perhaps a generation skipping trust. And definitely a Charitable Remainder Trust. Okay, got that?

On the business side of things it may be necessary to have a Buy-Out Agreement with your business partners, or perhaps your business would be best served by transferring ownership into a LLC or a corporation, or your family property or business into a FLC. (See *Transferring Family Wealth.*)

INQUIRING MINDS WANT TO KNOW

It is not the intention of this guidebook to be flippant with legal terms, like those above that sound like some archaic lexicon from ages past. But to a certain extent that is exactly what legal language is. It was never intended to be used in the vernacular, and it is near impossible to translate without losing meaning.

Nevertheless, the idea here is to breed familiarity with the language used in legal documents that will divide and distribute your estate after you or your spouse is gone. If you did not want to know more about the "terms of art" you would not be reading this.

At the risk of being criticized for oversimplifying the definitions of complex legal concepts, or perhaps applauded for doing the same, there are some terms you need to know to better understand how estate planning works.

Here are some brief descriptions of the terms mentioned above. To make it simpler assume stereotypically that Husband has died first. "Husband" computes much easier than the term "deceased Settlor."

91

"The Three-Way Formula Split With Marital Deduction Pecuniary Formula Clause":

You may think you will never run across a phrase like this in your estate plan, but in fact the clause is used frequently in Living Trusts. Its purpose is to determine how much of the deceased Husband's estate goes directly to the Wife, and how much of the estate assets will fund the Bypass Trust.

Generically speaking, a "marital deduction formula clause" splits the Husband's and Wife's estate into two parts: the marital deduction share that goes to the Wife's Survivor's Trust, and the nonmarital deduction share that goes into the deceased Husband's "credit shelter trust" e.g. Bypass Trust, to be used by Wife for her lifetime, then distributed to the children upon her death.

Remember that Wife is entitled by law to receive all of her Husband's estate directly into her Survivor's Trust when he dies and not pay a penny of taxes on it, even if it was a billion dollars. This is called the "unlimited marital deduction." (See *How The Federal Exemption Tax Works.*)

This "unlimited marital deduction exemption," as opposed to a "marital deduction formula clause" could produce horrendous results. It would be a very expensive mistake for Wife to accept all of her Husband's estate into her own estate because their children would pay a whopper of a tax on it when she dies.

The marital deduction formula clause divides the Husband's property between the Wife's Survivor's Trust and his Bypass Trust by using a formula. The most popular formula for dividing up the property interest is called a "pecuniary marital formula."

It is the most popular because it avoids many of the pitfalls created when dividing property by a fractional interest formula, or by direct gifting.

For example, if you split up Husband's estate fractionally with 1/2 of an asset going to the Survivor's Trust and 1/2 going to the Bypass Trust, you could end up with co-ownership of the asset between hostile family members.

Pecuniary means "money" and when Husband's estate is divided by a pecuniary formula it means that upon his death a certain amount of his monetary interest "under the formula" is going to be allocated to the Survivor's Trust, or the Bypass Trust, or even the QTIP Trust.

Unlike the fractional formula clause, the pecuniary formula clause allows the trustee to "pick and choose" the asset that will go into the specific trust. This means the asset must be valuated before it can be distributed to the trust, then it is put in one trust or the other as a whole.

The amount of pecuniary interest that will be allocated to the Survivor's Trust or the Bypass Trust will read something like this: "The trustee shall distribute to the Bypass Trust the smallest pecuniary amount so as to result in the least tax paid and produce the optimum marital deduction for the estate of the surviving spouse." The goal is to achieve the most favorable tax treatment.

This allows the trustee, Nora in the case of Dr. Dentist discussed above, to select specific assets from the estate after Dr. Dentist's death in order to fund the marital and nonmarital shares of the estate. She gets maximum flexibility of "picking and choosing" specific assets in order to get the best tax results. Not only does she allocate specific property to go into specific trusts, but she chooses which assets to keep for her own.

The major benefit is that she can efficiently tailor her share of the estate to receive the most favorable income tax results during her lifetime, and for her children after she is gone. She can also decide exactly which asset may best satisfy an individual beneficiary's needs (such as her two daughters) and put those assets into the Bypass Trust. These may be highly appreciating stocks that would only increase the size of Nora's estate unnecessarily.

Because Nora does not have to make the marital deduction election until after Dr. Dentist dies, she will have a clearer picture of the financial reality than what existed when she and the Dr. had the Will or Trust drafted.

A "three way formula split" is applicable where there is a Living Trust created by two married persons such as Dr. Dentist and Nora. Typically, when they establish their Living Trust, it will contain both their community property as well as their separate property. When Dr. Dentist dies it may be necessary to divide the Living Trust property into three shares.

When a three-way division is made, there will be a "marital deduction share," a "nonmarital share," and a "survivor's share" consisting of Nora's separate property plus her share of their community property. This three-way split preserves the distinction between Nora's property and the property that formerly belonged to Dr. Dentist. This facilitates different treatment of those two categories of property which is beyond the scope of this discussion.

But note! This three-way split may be more helpful to an estate like Walt the Plumber.

Since Walt recently remarried there has been no time to accumulate community property. We know he comes into the relationship with a substantial amount of separate property. If his new wife also came into the marriage with substantial separate property to leave to her family, then a three-way split may be the best way to organize the estate.

However, the "marital deduction pecuniary formula clause" has no place in the distribution of Walt's estate. It would not be advisable to leave the "picking and choosing" of his assets to the discretion of his new wife for the benefit of his children. Under normal conditions it is not the wise thing to do.

It would be best if Walt and his new wife entered into an "Agreement Between Spouses Regarding Status of Property." (See *When Death And Divorce Collide.*)

Disclaimer Trust

A marital deduction pecuniary clause, or "formula clause" and a disclaimer trust operate in much the same way. They both give Nora the advantage of "picking and choosing" assets she may or may not want in her own estate now that she is single.

The difference is that a "formula clause" controls how much of her husband's estate shall be distributed into each Bypass or QTIP trust, while a Disclaimer Trust allows her to keep her husband's entire estate if she so chooses.

Along with this power to choose comes the "power of appointment" allowing her to bequeath and devise her husband's share of the estate the way she wants. This power over her husband's assets also makes her vulnerable to the interpretation that the assets should be included back into her estate for tax purposes.

In our stereotypical example where Dr. Dentist dies first, a Disclaimer Trust is used to help the surviving Nora tailor her own estate to gain the most favorable income tax advantage. The Disclaimer Trust operates the same as a credit shelter trust (Bypass Trust) only it is funded differently.

Instead of the trust being irrevocably funded upon the death of Dr. Dentist by way of a marital deduction formula, Nora has the opportunity to decide how much of Dr. Dentist's share of the estate she wants to accept into her own estate, or how much of the property she doesn't accept (disclaims) because of the poor tax result to her surviving estate.

She would then pass the disclaimed property on to the Dr.'s credit shelter trust (now called a "Disclaimer Trust") and she could become a lifetime beneficiary of the trust income, as well as have a right to invade the principal of the trust.

The allure of the Disclaimer Trust is that it allows Nora to postpone the issue of the size of the "credit shelter trust" she will fund from her husband's estate, until after he dies. At the time they sign their Will or Living Trust there may be some uncertainty as to how large Dr. Dentist's separate estate may actually be years later when he's gone.

If his estate has downturns and is sufficiently small Nora may want it all to pass into her estate because there will be no significant tax result. But if it has substantially grown over the years she may want to disclaim a portion of it and put it in the credit shelter trust to preserve for herself, and perhaps "sprinkle" for the benefit of her children.

As a practical matter, the disclaimer trust should only be used if Nora has sufficient business acumen and expert financial advice to help make certain her choices on accepting or disclaiming property are the right ones.

Also, if Dr. Dentist has any concern that Nora's shopping habits may tempt her into accepting his entire estate into her own, and disclaiming none of the assets regardless of the tax results, then the Disclaimer Trust is a bad idea.

In the case of Dr. Dentist's a Disclaimer Trust would be a smart tool for their estate plan. But for Walt the plumber, he would certainly not need Wife #3 deciding which of his assets should go into her Survivor's Trust. Walt's goals would be better met by using a Bypass Trust with his children as beneficiaries, as well as a QTIP trust. (See *The Nuts And Bolts Of the Living Trust.*)

Family Pot Trust – with Sprinkling Powers or "Sprinkling Trust"

A good tool for a family like Dr. Dentist and Nora with two minor girls is the family pot trust. This trust pools together property for the benefit of their daughters into a single trust, as opposed to funding two separate trusts.

If the trustee is given "sprinkling power" over the distribution of trust assets, it means the trustee has full discretion to decide when to pay money, how much to pay, and what proportion of the trust to pay to each child.

The effect of allowing a trustee to "sprinkle" income and principal between the children is to substitute the same discretion as a parent. In this fashion, if both parents are deceased, the trustee has the power to provide for unforeseen crisis, or medical attention, or any other emergency.

The kind of flexibility provided in the "sprinkling power" allows the trustee to respond to the different needs of the children as they arise.

The trustee is otherwise limited to distributions of money to each child based on rigid trust formulas, or rules limiting distribution only from specific income property or only at a specific time. The family pot trust is thought to be a more fair way of distributing income to children.

Your children may all be loved the same, but they each have their own interest and ambitions as well as health and financial emergency needs. These needs require that various amounts of money be expended.

A family pot trust assures equal response to each child's unequal emergency needs, but it will make life difficult for the trustee who decides which emergency is more important than the other. (See *Another Word About Trustees.*)

A Sprinkling Trust "in three stages" is a family pot trust which begins to terminate when the youngest child has turned 18 or 20. In the case of two daughters, they would each receive an equal share portion of the trust as soon as the youngest turned 18.

A second sum may be distributed to each of them when the youngest turns 26, and the third and final portion of the trust would distributed to both sisters when the youngest reached age 30. However, the distribution ages are totally up to the parents.

Generation Skipping Trust – Not For Everybody

Do not confuse the "generation-skipping tax," with the "federal estate and gift tax." The "federal estate tax and gift tax" is a *unified* tax. The estate and gift tax draw from the same tax exemption.

To avoid paying the estate tax, you use the marital deduction exemption, and to not pay taxes on an annual gift to your child you use the annual gift tax exemption. (See *How The Federal Tax Exemption Works.*)

For example, if you died in the year 2006 your estate could exempt up to $2,000,000 and not pay any estate taxes on it.

But if during your lifetime you had made two annual gifts of $50,000 each, with each gift being $39,000 in excess of the annual gift tax deduction of $11,000 (you get an $11,000 deduction each year regardless of any more money you gift); and you took the tax credit of $50,000, for each of those years you made the gifts: then your "marital deduction exemption" of $2,000,000 would be reduced by the total of $78,000 for both the gifts, to $1,922,000. ($2,000,000 reduced by 2 years X a $39,000 overage of the $11,000 gift exemption allowed each year.)

The "generation-skipping tax" is a horse of a different color. It is only in very large estates where generation-skipping trusts are necessary to avoid paying the "federal generation-skipping transfer tax."

This is when tools such as the "reverse QTIP trust" can be used to obtain an "inclusion ratio of zero" (no tax) in order to not pay any taxes on the transfer. This practice as a desired goal is based entirely on the size of an individual's wealth, their expert tax representation, and personal desires.

How Badly Do You Want To Provide For Your Grandchildren?

Generation-skipping tax planning is usually for families that want to transfer their wealth tax-free to children for generations to come. Generation-skipping means leaving a portion of wealth for the third generation, such as if Walt the plumber wanted to leave special assets for his grandchildren.

But Walt's estate is probably not large enough to worry about generation skipping unless it is a priority for him. His desired results can be achieved by using other estate planning tools, while leaving his primary wealth to his second generation.

In extremely large estates, separate third generation-skipping trusts can be funded for each grandchild so that each grandchild's share is so large that it far exceeds all normally anticipated needs for their formative years. This is when there is truly enough money to go around.

This would not be Walt's concern. He has four adult children and a wife with whom to share his estate. He can provide for his grandchildren by first providing for his children whose share will, should they predecease Walt, go to that child's son or daughter.

Beyond the issue of wealth, a parent's desire to incur the complexities involved in a third generation trust is dependent upon their relationship with their grandchildren. The closer the relationship, the more inclined they are to incur the complexities.

Tax considerations play a part but do not rule the decision making process. Most grandparents usually do not consider themselves as owing an obligation of support to their grandchildren. A parent's primary concern is most often protecting their own children from squandering their inheritance at an early age.

WHEN DEATH AND DIVORCE COLLIDE

When Death And Divorce Collide – A Transmutation Wreck

What could be more depressing than a discussion about death and divorce? What is more heartbreaking? Anyone who has lost a family member, or lived through a divorce, knows the heartbreak of these events.

But for some, this trauma is exacerbated by in-fighting over property rights between parents, and/or between children; particularly between "blended family" members. The issue is the same whether the dispute arises out of death or divorce. The answer to who is entitled to reimbursement for money invested in specific family properties is found in the legal term, "transmutation of property."

"Transmutation" is the process by which the property rights of married persons are changed from separate property to community property, or vice versa. This transmutation may be done through written agreements between husband and wife for various reasons, including, but not limited to a great tax advantage upon the death of the first spouse as explained below.

Characterization of property at death is crucial because it identifies how much of the estate each spouse is allowed to pass on to his or her heirs. Husband and wife are each entitled to will, devise or bequest their 50% share of the community property to whomever they please, but they have 100% control over their separate property.

This is where death and divorce collide. There is a big difference between the transmutation of property when you are getting divorced and when you are determining ownership rights after death.

For divorce purposes, any separate property that was contributed to the marriage to purchase community property can be traced back, and the contributing party has a right to reimbursement upon divorce. (Family Code § 2640)

But this is not the law upon death. After death, transmutation becomes a permanent one-way transaction that is a non recognized event. This means that it cannot be undone, and the contributing party is not entitled to reimbursement!

This can create disappointing surprises for heirs to an otherwise well planned estate. It is not the purpose of this discussion to show how to resolve all the conflicts that may arise over ownership of property. These conflicts must be examined on a case by case basis and could only be avoided if people lived in an ideal attorney's world. This is where all potential liabilities are foreseen and all reasonable precautions are taken well in advance.

But even in cases where the intentions of the parties are clear, it doesn't mean it will work out that way. As one astute legal scholar observed, "There is something wrong in the law where justice enjoys the power of making odd results that hurt the expected person to benefit."

This is in reference to cases where separate property rights are held to be community property and children from a previous marriage are denied their inheritance; or where a father's gift to a daughter is denied because she was a step child from a prior marriage, even though he raised the child for twenty years. In order to avoid these types of injustices the married couple must take every opportunity to make their intentions as clear as possible.

In an ideal attorney's world all couples, prior to marriage, would sit down and begin preparing for their divorce. They would each put their separate property in a "separate property trust." In this fashion it would be difficult for them to commingle their funds without intentionally doing so.

A separate property trust would be a great property identifier and a much cleaner machine than a "premarital contractual agreement" (aka "prenuptial agreement").

A prenuptial agreement is a contract between the bride and groom that determines how their property will be characterized after they are married. It is also good evidence to show the parties' clear intentions at a later date.

But as with any property agreement between spouses it must honestly address issues about money and what happens upon death. (See *"Spousal Fiduciary Duty" Husbands and Wives Must Communicate – Truthfully.*) A "prenup" works particularly well when one spouse owns a closely held business corporation, or where a younger man marries an older woman, or where there are children from a previous marriage.

Transmutation Agreements Can Save Big Money; Or Not

(A Hot Tip On Transmuting Joint Tenancy)

Since we don't live in the ideal attorney's world where a couple starts planning for divorce when they get married, a typical couple works hard and commingles assets with little regard toward the characterization of their property.

But if, after careful consideration, they have decided to convert their separate property into community property, then a Transmutation Agreement acknowledging that new ownership can be of great benefit.

But *Beware!* An agreement converting separate property into community property is the first thing you want to revoke when considering divorce.

Otherwise, it is a good tool for a well planned estate. Assume that an attorney encourages a couple married for twenty-five years to transmute the ownership of their residence from "joint tenancy with right of survivorship" into community property to gain a tax advantage upon the death of the first spouse.

For example, if the couple purchased a home in 1986 for $600,000 and in 2006 the home was worth $2,000,000 (not uncommon in California) each of the couple's half (50%) of the cost basis would be $300,000.

If the husband died, and the property was still held in joint tenancy, his 50% of cost basis ($300,000) would "step up" to $1,000,000 (50% fair market value at the time of death) but wife's cost basis would remain at $300,000. If wife sold the property she would pay taxes on $700,000. Because the couple received only a 50% step-up the survivor missed a significant tax savings opportunity.

But if the couple had entered into a Transmutation Agreement converting ownership of the residence to community property, then upon her husband's death the 50% cost basis she would receive from him would "step up" to $1,000,000 (same as above), **and** her cost basis on the half she owned would *also* "step up" to $1,000,000 (50% fair market value).

With a combined cost basis of $2,000,000, there would be no recognized gain on the sale and she would pay no taxes!

This would be wise estate planning in the event of death, but what if the couple was getting divorced the next year and Husband died? Would the attorney get sued for malpractice by his heirs?

Who Polices Property Agreements, Trust Properties, And Tax Advantages?

The short answer as to who polices these trust transactions is the IRS. Tax statements must be filed and the IRS has three years to uncover fraud or mistake.

In reality, the integrity of the trust business is regulated by the attorneys and CPA's that are charged with the job. Much of an attorney's continuing education in estate planning deals with ethical duties and obligations to the client. (See *Some Ethical considerations, e.g. Who Does Your Attorney Represent?*)

The relationship between client and attorney is extremely confidential. You must be able to confide in him or her and fully expect them to protect what they have heard in private. This is the only way to develop the kind of relationship necessary to get the job done right.

CHARITABLE REMAINDER UNITRUST

The Best Trust On The Market

The "Charitable Remainder Unitrust" is a gift from the government that rewards your philanthropy. You give to the charity of your choice when you die, and the government gives you your tax dollars while you live. It trades charity for tax dollars.

There is no trust more giving or more receiving than the charitable remainder unitrust. It has flexible terms and conditions, and is adaptable to any taxpayer with a highly appreciated asset and a very low cost basis.

For example, a rental property purchased for $200,000 which is now worth $1,000,000 or a stock share that is presently worth $100 but was purchased for $2.00, are the types of highly appreciated assets that make a good corpus for a trust. In other words, wherever there is an enormous capital gains tax looming, there is a need for a charitable remainder unitrust.

The charitable remainder unitrust (CRUT) is an irrevocable trust that defers your donation to charity, and gives you the immediate benefit of the tax deduction, and a specified sum of money paid annually, quarterly or monthly until the "remainder" becomes due. The best way to describe the benefits of a CRUT is to give an example of how it works.

Assume that a 65 year-old gentleman named Fritz has a stock portfolio worth $600,000. Fritz purchased these stocks back in the '70's for $5,000. If he sold the stock today he would pay the capital gains tax on $595,000 at about 15% Federally, and 9.3% California State capital gains tax. That would be $144,585 in taxes.

Because of this huge tax consequence, rather than sell his stocks Fritz has been living off the margin of his stock account. This means he has been borrowing money against the value of his stocks from his brokerage firm at a rate of about 8% interest. Paying the 8% interest on borrowed income is better than paying the 24.3% state and federal capital gains tax he would have to pay by selling the stocks. Afterall, the stocks continue to increase in value and make him money.

Many older people in Fritz's position live off the margin of their securities account. If they are old enough they simply outlive the amount of money they can borrow on the account. It is a good strategy if all the numbers work out right.

This way there is never a taxable event to gouge their estate from much needed funds for living. When they die the margin account dies with them and they never have to pay taxes on their much appreciated stock profit that they have been using for living expenses. That's one way to save.

But Fritz is not that old or that rich. His margin account is now maxed out at $100,000 and the brokerage house is demanding payment.

In order to pay back the $100,000 loan, Fritz has to sell nearly $135,000 worth of stock. This is because $32,805 of that sale would go to federal and state taxes. To get $100,000 Fritz has to pay $32,805 more in taxes. That's a bad deal.

However, because Fritz is 65 years old, a smart alternative would be for him to donate the $135,000 to his favorite charity, the "Fiesta Foundation," through a Charitable Remainder Unitrust. This CRUT will pay Fritz 5% of the CRUT's value every year for life. More importantly, the contribution will create an income tax deduction in the year of contribution of $63,107 (according to the IRS tables and interest rates of January, 2006).

Using this tax deduction Fritz would only need to sell $111,843 in securities (not $135,000) to have $100,000 left after taxes to pay the margin loan. Using the tax benefit of the CRUT he is able to payoff the margin loan at a cost of $11,843 in taxes vs. $32,805 in taxes.

Referring to the CRUT's immediate "tax benefit" or "tax credit" can be misleading in the sense that the contribution to the CRUT does not provide a "dollar for dollar" reduction in tax. The contribution of the property to the CRUT provides a tax deduction toward "computing" taxable income, and therefore the income tax is lower. (The exact tax credit is determined by a complicated IRS formula crossing age and life expectancy with valuation tables, interest rate, etc.)

To eliminate taxes entirely on selling his stock to payoff the margin, Fritz would have to contribute $214,000 to the CRUT. This would provide a $100,000 tax deduction (instead of the $63,107 tax deduction above) enabling $100,000 of his securities to be sold to pay off the margin loan. (Again, refer to your CPA's IRS tax tables.)

At the end of the year Fritz will have paid off his margin account, have $214,000 in his CRUT, and will have paid NO TAXES on the appreciated and/or sold stocks in the CRUT. However, Fritz, or any other recipient of the CRUT distribution funds, is taxed on the money they receive from the CRUT as personal income.

Fritz will be the sole beneficiary of the CRUT for life, and he will receive quarterly payments from the CRUT to supplement his other earned income. The stocks in the CRUT can continue to appreciate at a meteoric rate and there will never be any income tax to pay on the capital gains until they are distributed. All CRUT gains are income tax exempt!

But now comes the best part. As sole beneficiary to the CRUT, Fritz is entitled to a specified percentage of at least 5% of the net market value of the CRUT, each year for life.

There is some flexibility in the distribution percentage of this yearly sum because like the tax benefit above, the exact amount of money Fritz will be paid is determined by a formula on a software program.

But when the trust is terminated, such as when Fritz dies, and the donation to the charity (termed the "remainder") becomes due, the minimum net value of trust assets that goes to the "Fiesta Foundation" is ten percent; and in some cases only five percent.

Ten percent of $214,000 is $21,400. That's a good deal for both Fritz and the Fiesta Foundation. Meanwhile, the stock in the CRUT may appreciate two or three times over, if Fritz is very, very lucky.

By examining the benefits that Fritz received from the Charitable Remainder Unitrust, you can extrapolate on how those benefits might apply to your own financial legacy. The CRUT, as a deferred giving tool can be very versatile and serve many purposes when used with a little imagination.

As another example, if Husband (and of course vice versa) wants to provide for the security of Wife, he could put that $2,000,000 piece of appreciated property he's been holding into a Charitable Remainder Unitrust and sell it tax free.

Then over the next twenty years the CRUT could pay out $90,000 (or more or less) a year to Wife for her sole benefit from the $2,000,000 sale. Also, the $2,000,000 that goes into the CRUT is deducted from the gross value of their estate and therefore isn't counted for estate tax purposes at death, as long as the trust terminates at death. (If there is a successor trustee then only a portion is excluded.)

In deciding whether or not to use a CRUT just add up the tax advantages along with the life time benefits, and the benefit to your charity. It may help you sleep at night. For many people it is the best option for the family and for posterity at the same time.

College Savings Trusts

Another example of a Charitable Remainder Trust is an "annuity trust." This charitable remainder "trust" is different from the "unitrust" because it provides a specific amount of money to the beneficiary for a specific amount of time – like money to your daughter during her four (five?) years in college.

Let's assume that Fritz has a daughter named Debby who is about to enter college. He wants to do something *smart* to help pay for her education, and something *good* for his favorite charity.

Fritz decides to take $100,000 of stock out of his brokerage account in the same year Debby is starting college, and puts it in a Charitable Remainder Trust (CRT).

In the CRT the stocks can appreciate or be liquidated without creating a taxable event just like the CRUT, and the funds in the trust are tax exempt. Fritz has also avoided the capital gains tax he would otherwise have paid had he simply sold the stocks to pay for Debby's education.

Fritz decides to use a five year term for the annuity trust to make payouts to Debby (by the end of college she calls herself Deborah). At the specified percentage rate of 18% per year, Deborah will receive $18,000 (or a little less each year as the trust value diminishes) while in college, and one year after college. One *caveat*, the $18,000 is taxable to Debby.

That totals the sum of $90,000 to Deborah, and if the trust averages 8% interest per year, Fritz's favorite trust, the "Fiesta Foundation" will receive approximately $50,000 after five years. That is a win, win, win situation, for Deborah, Fritz *and* his Fiesta Foundation.

Something to always remember when planning for your child's college education is that the assets that fund the Charitable Remainder Trust are income tax exempt. That means the original $100,000 asset can be sold and reinvested, and bought and diversified and sold again and again without any tax ramifications.

This makes it much easier to accumulate wealth. Therefore, if Debby's CRT is started when she is five, there are thirteen years to build her college fund. The ten percent that must remain in the trust for charity only applies to the original net value of the trust. The rest of the value in the trust is accumulated wealth.

The 529 Plan College Savings Plan

When considering college savings plans it is worth mentioning a "529 Plan." In California this state-run savings program is called the "ScholarShare Trust." It is administered by a state agency called the "ScholarShare Investment Board" which began accepting investments in 1999.

Similar to programs in other states, the purpose of this trust is to help people save money for college. Saving is encouraged by the plan's enhanced State and Federal tax benefits, and is as easy as opening a bank account.

The ScholarShare Trust is a "hands off" investment for contributors and is managed by a professional investment firm for a .80% fee. The 529 Plan's best feature is that the earned income from the savings is tax exempt. When the funds are distributed (for college use only!) the student will not pay any income tax on the earned income.

Contributing to California's 529 Plan is the same as opening a savings account with the "Golden State" and you can do so with as little as $25.00. There are various investment plans to choose from, but the investment is not federally insured and can fluctuate with the market.

As with any gift plan, you can contribute up to $11,000 each year without having to file a gift tax return and can contribute up to $285,000 overall in California. Some of the investment options are guaranteed and some are not. It is highly advisable that you check with a tax advisor before contributing to a 529 Plan. For more information go to ScholarShare.com.

119

FAMILY WEALTH TRANSFERS THROUGH BUSINESS ENTITIES.

Transferring Family Wealth Using FLPs And LLCs.

"Family Limited Partnerships" and "Limited Liability Partnerships" are legal entities into which older family members can transfer ownership of wealth to younger family members with enhanced tax savings.

But if you ever wanted to get paranoid about the IRS and their recent move to uncover FLPs and LLCs as vehicles for fraudulent transfers, just spend a day with an IRS tax attorney and let him count the ways.

These transfers are commonly suspect when donors retain too much management and control, or coincidentally transfer and sell their assets immediately before death.

When the guilty get busted, the assets are transferred back into the donor's estate and the participants are penalized under IRC §§ 2038, 2036 and the newly developed Reg. 230 – all of which is way beyond the scope of this guidebook. The penalty is normally 20%.

Much of the controversy centers on "valuation discounts" and whether the transaction's "principle purpose" is tax avoidance, or whether its "significant purpose" is tax avoidance.

In simple language, you cannot put your house or business in a partnership just to transfer a "minor interest" in ownership to your children to avoid taxes. There must be a legitimate business interest for creating the business entity.

As a point of relative interest, IRS Reg. 230 is directly related to the "disclaimer" boldly set forth in the front of this booklet. The disclaimer assures the reader that no opinion herein is a "marketed opinion" and no information provided can be used to avoid tax penalties for which the taxpayer would otherwise be responsible.

This disclaimer is necessary to make sure some dummy doesn't get into trouble with the IRS and blame the author of this material for giving him illegal tax advice. The standard taxpayer's excuse for cheating on his/her taxes is, "I reasonably relied on my professional."

But for the sake of general knowledge a FLP, disparagingly referred to by the IRS as a "vanilla flip" is a Family Limited Partnership where investors hold partnership shares, and a LLC is a Limited Liability Company where investors hold membership shares.

They are both legal entities into which you can transfer wealth such as business interest, stocks, real estate holdings, etc., and they both provide creditor protection for legitimate business purposes.

A primary objective of all estate planning is to preserve and transfer wealth from one generation to the next with the least possible transfer cost, i.e. taxes before and/or after death.

In the mid 1980's the "tax shelter industry" began to remove assets from their client's large estates and transfer them into a FLP or LLC where both the parents and children were investors.

For starters this reduces the size of the parent's estate for estate tax purposes. It also allows for the value of the assets to be transferred to younger family members with the tax advantage of greatly reduced value through the manipulation of "valuation discounts" and "liquidation rights."

Do not be concerned with these discounts and rights unless you are very serious about transferring large amounts of stock, or realty or business shares to your children while you are alive.

To take proper advantage of these types of opportunities you need a good tax attorney, a CPA, and an "expert" appraiser in determining discounts for lack of control and lack of marketability for "fractional interest" in real property and for interest in business entities

(FLPs, LLCs) which hold traditional and non-traditional assets.

If The Above Sounds Like Gobbledygook, Read This

The use of different business entities to transfer appreciated property between family members has increasingly become more common and in many cases fundamental to estate planning.

There are many forms of business entities to choose from when parents want to move their commercial property or family business into a form of co-ownership with their children.

As older family members give ownership to younger family members they receive what is called "valuation discounts" on the property as determined by appraisers, and this saves them tax dollars.

Example: Mom and Dad have a six-plex apartment house purchased ten years ago for $200,000, now worth $1,000,000. Junior and Sis' are 18 and 19 years old. Mom and Dad want to introduce them into the world of apartment management and help develop their business acumen.

They want to do it gradually by transferring control and management of ownership over the years. They also want to reduce the tax liability of transferring ownership, as opposed to outright gifting it.

These are some of their business entity options:

1. <u>Tenancy in common.</u> This is where each family member owns a piece of the whole. But the ownership interest is cumbersome and it is difficult to establish ownership transfers. Because of the restrictions of ownership for tenants in common it does not allow "minority interest" (Junior and Sis's interest) to do with the property what they want. This can result in family litigation, such as a right to partition, which could lead to a "cloud on the title," let alone a cloud on the family.

2. <u>Trusts.</u> There are many types of trusts to choose from but these are not always the best choice. Each one brings with it the duty of fiduciary powers and special tax considerations. Also each trust has regulations regarding the beneficiaries that may not allow the desired freedom that was intended.

3. <u>Corporations.</u> A corporation must follow strict regulations, but more importantly this form of entity is inflexible in getting funds out of the corporation. Donors (Mom and Dad) are also subject to double taxation where, for example, they transfer their car to the corporation and have to pay tax on its use, or where they sell highly appreciated assets through the corporation then have to pay both corporate and personal income tax. These problems are impractical along with commingling of funds.

4. <u>General Partnership or Joint Venture.</u> These partnerships are convenient but offer nothing in terms of tax advantage or credit protection.

5. <u>Limited Partnership vs. Limited Liability Company</u>:

The "Limited Partnership" was once the preferred business entity for owning family property, or business. It still is popular where there is a preferred distinction between two classes of investors.

The difference between a Limited Partnership and a LLC is that an LP *always* has two tiers of partnership interest. There are the limited partners and the general partners. The limited partners have no hand in management and the general partners are the managers of the business enterprise.

Therefore the general partners can be held personally liable for the negligent acts or business failures of the organization and the limited partners cannot.

Because of this vulnerability to personal liability general partners were often cloaked in the protection of a corporate entity. This meant it was not Mom and Dad who were the general partners of the partnership, but Mom and Dad, Inc.

This way it was Mom and Dad's corporate identity that was open to direct liability from creditors and their personal assets remained safely veiled behind the corporate structure. (So long as they followed all the corporate rules.)

As clever a relationship as this was, it nevertheless created problems to have multiple entities as part of the same partnership, not the least of which was accounting for the corporate and partnership income.

The "Limited Liability Company" is now the preferred business entity in California for holding real property or a family business. Investors are called "members." Unless the articles of organization of the LLC state otherwise, the business affairs of the company are "member managed," and there are no separate classes of investors.

This allows for great management flexibility because management can be as decentralized, democratic or informal as a general partnership; or alternatively, the LLC can adopt a corporate style of management with a board of directors and managers; or alternatively, if the articles of organization call for it the LLC can adopt a management style analogous to a limited partnership.

The best feature is that members of an LLC are not personally liable for the debts, obligation, or liabilities of the LLC solely by reason of being a member. Mom, Dad, Junior, and Sis' all have limited liability. This limited liability protects members regardless of whether the liability arises in contract, tort or otherwise.

But there are exceptions to this rule of limited liability and members may be held personally liable if a court "pierces the company veil" of the LLC. This is similar to "piercing the corporate veil" but the court does not consider the failure to hold member or manager meetings or failure to observe other formalities because, hopefully, your attorney did not put such formalities in your operating agreement.

As for transferring financial interest, the LLC member can transfer their financial interest without the consent of others. Therefore when

Junior gets older and wants to cash out to become an artist, he can sell his membership interest, but, as with all partnerships, he can only sell his interest in the right to distribution of profit or loss, not voting or management rights – although that may be of little consolation to Mom and Dad.

The LLC is also attractive because of pass-through tax treatment to the members, and it avoids the double taxation issue of a corporation. The downside in California is that an LLC, as well as a limited liability company, is subject to an annual tax of $800.00.

Do You Want To Gamble Your Life Term Against The IRS Actuary Tables?

Feeling lucky? Here is a legitimate way to put your residence into a trust and transfer ownership to your children at a huge tax advantage – providing you live long enough.

It is called a Qualified Personal Residence Trust (QPRT). The IRS allows you to bet that you will outlive their actuary tables. Say you are 60 years old. You put your residence (or vacation home) in an irrevocable trust naming your children as final beneficiaries after a term of (your choice) 15 years.

If you live long enough to see your kids own your house, you not only get full ownership rights to your house for those 15 years, but a big reduction by the IRS on the gift tax, *and* the residence is not included in your estate tax upon your death!

The term of the trust is up to you, but the older you are and the longer the term of the trust, the bigger the IRS tax credit.

Of course you are 15 years older now and you no longer own your home.

If you do not outlive the 15 year term of the trust, the residence is added back into your estate and there is no added benefit. It is simply a lost opportunity and you are out the money for the formation of the trust, except, of course, you are not alive.

The QPRT is actually a good deal but it has to be done for the right reasons. Those reasons include:

- A desire to see the children enjoy the house;
- To help develop your heirs asset base;
- To provide needed support while relieving your own financial burden; and/or
- To protect assets from your or your children's creditors.

There are many other reasons to gift your assets to your heirs but tax reduction should not be the main reason. Too many things can go wrong between the gifting and the afterlife.

Many of us between the ages of 45 and 65 have children who believe they have a right of entitlement to exactly what their parents have and they want it now. The law books are filled with cases of children suing their parents for their share of the "partnership" because they do not want to wait for their inheritance.

If your children are not like that, fine, but it is something of a national epidemic. Children in their 30's and 40's are moving back home. In the case of choosing a QPRT you never know until it's too late if you can trust your children because the trust is irrevocable.

For that reason, the QPRT, and its cousins the GRAT and the GRIT, are only recommended to those parents, or single persons that feel comfortable with their heirs, and are relying on very sound tax advice.

If you believe your estate will be within the allotted tax exemption limit when you, or both you and your spouse die, then there is no need to consider it.

REEXAMINE DR. DENTIST AND WALT THE PLUMBER

Now that everything has been covered from "transmutation agreements," to "disclaimer trust," to "limited liability companies," it's time to reexamine the flow charts depicting the estate strategies of Dr. Dentist and Walt the Plumber. Starting with the two basic plans, look at the follow up pages showing the types of notes you should be writing on the charts to figure out your own strategy.

All of the flow charts in this book can be found in chronological order in the Appendix, to give you a feel for the entire web of estate planning ideas. If you take the time to study them, and reflect on their virtues and their shortcomings, you'll begin to feel like you know what you are talking about. As soon as that happens, you are ready to talk with an attorney.

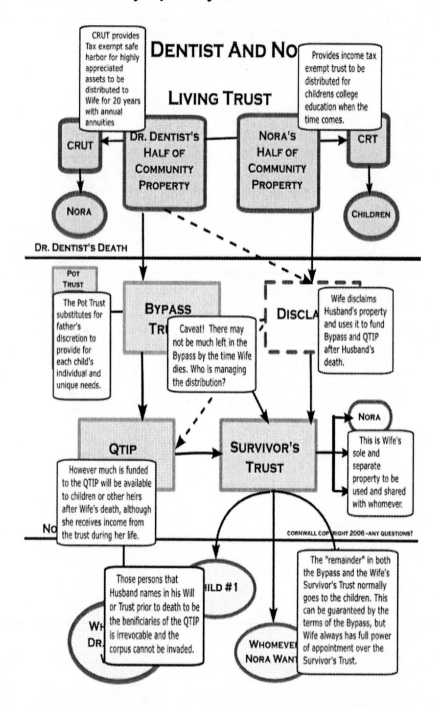

DENTIST AND NO

LIVING TRUST

CRUT provides Tax exempt safe harbor for highly appreciated assets to be distributed to Wife for 20 years with annual annuities

Provides income tax exempt trust to be distributed for childrens college education when the time comes.

CRUT

DR. DENTIST'S HALF OF COMMUNITY PROPERTY

NORA'S HALF OF COMMUNITY PROPERTY

CRT

NORA

CHILDREN

DR. DENTIST'S DEATH

POT TRUST

The Pot Trust substitutes for father's discretion to provide for each child's individual and unique needs.

BYPASS TR

Caveat! There may not be much left in the Bypass by the time Wife dies. Who is managing the distribution?

DISCLA

Wife disclaims Husband's property and uses it to fund Bypass and QTIP after Husband's death.

QTIP

However much is funded to the QTIP will be available to children or other heirs after Wife's death, although she receives income from the trust during her life.

SURVIVOR'S TRUST

NORA

This is Wife's sole and separate property to be used and shared with whomever.

Those persons that Husband names in his Will or Trust prior to death to be the benificiaries of the QTIP is irrevocable and the corpus cannot be invaded.

HILD #1

WH

DR.

WHOMEVE NORA WANT

The "remainder" in both the Bypass and the Wife's Survivor's Trust normally goes to the children. This can be guaranteed by the terms of the Bypass, but Wife always has full power of appointment over the Survivor's Trust.

CORNWALL COPYRIGHT 2006 –ANY QUESTIONS?

132

WALT THE PLUMBING CONTRACTOR

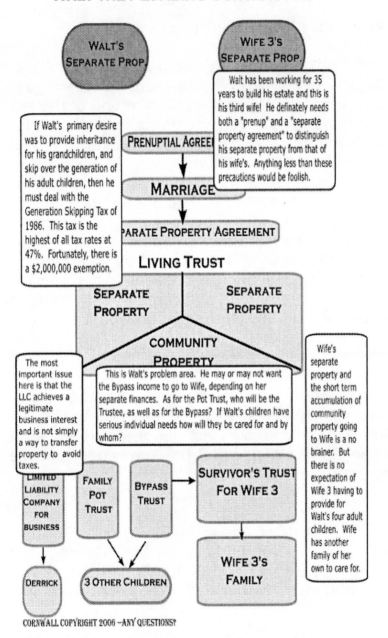

WALT'S SEPARATE PROP.

WIFE 3'S SEPARATE PROP.

Walt has been working for 35 years to build his estate and this is his third wife! He definately needs both a "prenup" and a "separate property agreement" to distinguish his separate property from that of his wife's. Anything less than these precautions would be foolish.

If Walt's primary desire was to provide inheritance for his grandchildren, and skip over the generation of his adult children, then he must deal with the Generation Skipping Tax of 1986. This tax is the highest of all tax rates at 47%. Fortunately, there is a $2,000,000 exemption.

PRENUPTIAL AGREE

MARRIAGE

ARATE PROPERTY AGREEMENT

LIVING TRUST

SEPARATE PROPERTY

SEPARATE PROPERTY

COMMUNITY PROPERTY

The most important issue here is that the LLC achieves a legitimate business interest and is not simply a way to transfer property to avoid taxes.

This is Walt's problem area. He may or may not want the Bypass income to go to Wife, depending on her separate finances. As for the Pot Trust, who will be the Trustee, as well as for the Bypass? If Walt's children have serious individual needs how will they be cared for and by whom?

Wife's separate property and the short term accumulation of community property going to Wife is a no brainer. But there is no expectation of Wife 3 having to provide for Walt's four adult children. Wife has another family of her own to care for.

LIMITED LIABILITY COMPANY FOR BUSINESS

FAMILY POT TRUST

BYPASS TRUST

SURVIVOR'S TRUST FOR WIFE 3

DERRICK

3 OTHER CHILDREN

WIFE 3'S FAMILY

LITIGATION

You Don't Want It, But...

Make no mistake about it; you do not want litigation. Sitting in a courtroom below the judge, with your brother at the opposite end of the table, and fighting over your mother's family home is not what you want to do. It is hateful.

On the other hand, things happen. Perhaps in your mother's last couple of months your brother's wife went every day and helped her through her sickness. Perhaps she cooked and cared and cleaned for her. And as your mother became more ill and the dosages of her medicine became more potent, she came to only recognize your sister-in-law as the person who loved her most.

So she had your sister-in-law make an appointment with her old attorney and on a day she was feeling pretty good she went to the attorney, escorted by her daughter-in-law, and changed her Will so that the family home was left to your brother and his wife, and you were left only $25,000.

This may come as quite a shock after the funeral when you find out, particularly when the house is worth $1,000,000, and particularly when you and your brother had previously talked about how you would each receive equal shares. What would you do?

First, you would probably try and talk to your brother, but when he told you to go pound sand what would you do? Maybe you would go to an attorney and tell him he could use your entire inheritance of $25,000 to fight this inequity, you just want your half of the house.

There would be a problem with this arrangement immediately. The Will no doubt would have a "no contest clause" meaning that if you contest the Will you will not be eligible to receive the $25,000 inheritance– if you lose.

Playing To Win Cost More Than Money

Perhaps you decide to take the risk and put up your own $25,000 to fight the Will. Your attorney advises you that you have a pretty good case. Afterall, your mother was very ill at the time and under the influence of drugs and could have been incompetent to rewrite her Will. Her state of mind would have to be examined. Neighbors and friends would have to be interviewed. Her doctor would have to be deposed, as well as her attorney, and the sister-in-law, and of course your brother.

At each one of these depositions, which cost lots of money, you will be sitting in a constant state of anxiety and despair each time someone testifies under oath how sane your mother was up until the day of her death. The tension in the room when your brother and his wife are deposed will make you feel sick every time they lie to support their own cause.

But if your attorney is good enough he will make them feel even worse. Hopefully, their minds will fill with doubt about whether it is worth proceeding. They have to pay for their attorney the same as you, only their desire to win is not fueled by the same desire that burns in you from feeling deceived.

Meanwhile, the attorneys are going to court on a regular basis and fighting over every little thing that surrounds your mother's estate and the need for information. Motions are made to seek and destroy the opposition while the cost of litigation just keeps going up.

The best you can hope for at this point is that the other side has had enough and will throw in the towel. This is much easier for them to do in a contested Will case because the money was not theirs in the first place. It's much easier to give up something you never had, and if their decision is to give you half of the home that was never theirs then your attorney has done an outstanding job.

If the case goes to trial, it is impossible to say who will win. The arguments are strong on both sides but in a probate case, which is what this is, the facts are heard and decided upon by a Judge. What that Judge believes and how he reads the evidence is anybody's guess. That is why you want to stay out of court.

DOMESTIC PARTNERS

For Those Who Don't Know

On September 19, 2003 California passed into law Assembly Bill 205 known as the California Domestic Partners Rights and Responsibilities Act of 2003. It was designed to accommodate the over 100,000 households in California headed by same sex partners. It also benefits older heterosexual couples, where one partner is over 62 years old and looking for an alternative to marriage.

However, the word "benefit" in this context must be used carefully. The Act provides exactly what the name implies, which is rights *and* "responsibilities." But the responsibilities may be more than those persons living an unconventional lifestyle have bargained for, and the rights may be far less than they had hoped for.

Since the law only became fully operative on January 1, 2005, every case has to be analyzed individually. There is a dearth of case law to help attorneys advise clients, and the tax ramifications must be submitted to tax experts in this new field of practice.

The purpose of the law is to confer same sex couples the same equality and status as the spousal rights conferred on married couples. But it doesn't turn out that way for many same sex couples.

Denial Of Federal Benefits

On a Federal level the state status of a "domestic partner" has been preempted by what is known as the Defense of Marriage Act Statutes, or DOMA. Also passed by 40 other states, the Federal DOMA holds that the California Domestic Partnership Act has no bearing on the federal definition of "marriage" or "spouse," and will not qualify domestic partners for Section 1138 federal benefits that accompany traditional marriages between a man and a woman.

In plain language this means that Federal Rights normally granted to a "spouse" are denied to Domestic Partners. This includes:

- Social Security Benefits to a surviving spouse;

- Veteran's Benefits such as disability, dependency or death benefits to spouses;

- Tax Consequences: 179 provisions of tax law including the unlimited marital deduction upon the first spouse's death! (See *How The Federal Tax Exemption Works.*)

- Employment Protection: No entitlement to ERISA.

Depending on your status these denials could work against you if in deciding to be a stay-at-home partner you thought you would be eligible for your partner's federal pension.

Welcome To The World Of State Benefits

California's law is one of the most far-reaching in the country. Couples who qualify by registering with the Secretary of State are entitled to equal state-conferred rights regarding the following benefits. They all carry heavy responsibility:

- Financial support, including "spousal" (partner) support;

- Mutual responsibility for debts to third parties;

- Access to Superior Court for dissolution of relationship;

- Standing to assert legal claims based on marital status and employment rights for family care, medical and bereavement leave;

- Child custody and visitation, and child support;

- Communication privileges, including the right not to testify against your partner; and

Most importantly, for Estate Planning purposes, a domestic partner gets an identifiable status in Probate court. You are no longer a "stranger at law" with no status. You take the place of the "spouse" in the scheme of intestate succession. (See *Intestate Succession.*)

Previously, family members could attack this non status partnership as collusion for fraud, or make serious accusations regarding coercion and undue influence to receive inheritance.

The domestic partner now has a right to oversee their deceased partner's remains, including anatomical gifts, consent to autopsy, and burial in family cemeteries.

A Domestic Partnership Is Not A Political Statement

There are so many uncertainties in this new law that it is difficult to advocate that someone should register without first examining their needs and expectations very closely.

Entering into a domestic partnership is definitely not something you do to make a political statement. Anybody that signed up to support the gay and lesbian rainbow coalition at the park rally years ago is in for a rude awakening.

You could register in the year 2000 and in 2003 the law was passed, but it did not become operative until 2005. Then the law was made retroactive so that everyone who signed up was now legally bound to the partnership. All the rules and regulations regarding community property rights apply, and a divorce is necessary to dissolve the obligation.

As a practical matter this means some people didn't even know they were legally bound to each other, let alone that half of their earned income over the last five years belonged to their domestic partner.

Another concern is the fact that the jobless partner could now take the hard working partner to court and receive half the community estate going back for perhaps as long as they were domiciled together.

Bottom Line For Domestic Partners

The law essentially defines domestic partners as single persons with community property.

ELDER LAW

Who Does Elder Law Affect?

Elder law affects all those persons that are closest to us – all of the most precious people in our lives. This means your mother and father, grandpa and grandma, and everyone else in the family circle, including neighbors and friends. And yes, it will some day include you.

All of these people deserve respect and are entitled to be treated with dignity. For that reason the practice of elder law has a much more personal side to it than any other field of legal expertise.

Clients are normally introduced to elder law as a result of one of their older family members beginning to lose "capacity" to think for themselves. This does not mean all the time; they have good days and bad days, but gradually the symptoms of dementia are creeping into their lives.

Dementia does not mean "incapacitated." The term "good days and bad days" should not be underestimated. In many cases the elderly may not be suffering dementia at all. They may only seem temporarily incompetent due to symptoms of their medication, or depression, anxiety, or other mental disorder; or perhaps some visceral disease, or diabetes or cancer or infection.

The list goes on and it is important to consider these causes before jumping to the conclusion your father needs to execute a power of attorney naming you as his "agent" to handle all business and personal affairs. Before any such steps are taken your father should, quite literally, have his head examined. If he is not competent to sign a power of attorney you will have to seek a conservatorship.

Undue Influence Of A Caregiver

There is an entire history of undue influence and abuse which is the basis of the "Elder Abuse Laws." All of it surrounds the issue of an older person's "competency" and another person's undue influence on the incompetent. Listed below are many of the acts used as tell-tale signs of undue influence by a caregiver:

- Withholding mail;

- Withholding telephone messages;

- Limiting visitation by friends and family;

- Discussing transactions at inappropriate times and places;

- Obtaining access to bank accounts;

- Being named on a Power of Attorney;
- Using victim's property;

- Is the victim's only source of friendship; and

- Demanding business be terminated quickly.

Needless to say, whenever a caregiver ends up with property that would otherwise have gone to the victim's family the caregiver is going to be suspected of "abuse."

However, if the family waits until the elder dies before they take action, they may be prevented, or at least dissuaded from bringing a lawsuit because it would violate the "no contest clause" in the elder's Will. (There are ways around this but it is costly.)

It is interesting to note the profile of the "typical" abuser. Lawyers are on notice to beware of that 42 year old single son or daughter that is living at home and taking care of their surviving parent. He/she is the child that things never quite worked out for. Their siblings are busy doing other things and there is no one the victim feels they can trust more than their own child.

Capacity To Sign Power Of Attorney Or Health Care Directive

The biggest issue in any elder law case is going to be whether or not the Mom or Dad, aunt, uncle, grandma, grandpa or the neighbor next door had the "competency" or "capacity" (the terms are used interchangeably) to sign the documents distributing power or property at the "time" they signed the documents.

There are three levels of capacity:

1. Testamentary capacity;
2. Contractual capacity; and
3. Donor Capacity.

Of these three capacities "testamentary" requires the least amount of competency and "donor" requires the most.

"Testamentary power" is necessary for a person to sign a valid Will. It means they are able to, a.) Verify they know what property they own, i.e. the extent of their bounty, and b.) Understand the natural objects of their bounty, i.e. can identify their family members who would normally inherit their property.

"Contractual capacity" is necessary to sign a Durable Power of Attorney or Health Care Directive. This capacity requires the person be able to communicate, understand, and appreciate the decision at issue and the significant benefits, risk, and alternatives of that decision.

"Donor capacity" is that capacity required when you start putting your estate into an irrevocable trust or giving it away to your caregiver. You really need to know what you are doing!

Planning For Medi-Cal (Medic-Aid) For Long Term Care

Assume that your father whom you love so dearly is beginning to "wander" as he becomes increasingly unable to manage his affairs due to Alzheimer's disease. He is going to need long term health care in a skilled nursing facility, or perhaps even a "secure parameter facility." That is one of every family's worse nightmares. The average time spent in such a facility is three years. The average expense is $4,000 to $7,000 per month.

In preparation for such a calamity it is widely assumed that a person with substantial assets would not be eligible for the federally funded health insurance program. This is known as "Medic-Aid" throughout the United States, but is called "Medi-Cal" in California. Owning assets does not disqualify a person from Medi-Cal.

It is important for everyone to understand that Medi-Cal benefits can be available for almost every Baby Boomer as long as steps are taken to plan for it; and it is not too late to plan for your parents.

The money from Medi-Cal is a "loan" from the state which is to be paid back from the beneficiary's personal estate. The goals for an attorney in Medi-Cal planning are threefold:

First is to use Medi-Cal as a means to getting a client an immediate reduction in their cost for a skilled nursing facility. If their cost is $7,000 a month, the Medi-Cal benefits may be approximately $3,000 per month, saving the patient $4,000 per month.

Secondly, the goal is to reduce the patient's cost for skilled nursing care down to $0.00 if possible.

Third, the goal is to protect the patient's spouse from creditor claims and in any case to get the amount of money to be paid back to the state as low as possible.

Moral Issues?

There may be some moral issues regarding a beneficiary's responsibility to pay the money back to the state; or to the fact that an applicant may have transferred property out of their estate in the first place to become eligible for Medi-Cal. But California has a liberal policy regarding these issues and it can only be expected that a client will use the laws available to them.

For example, the state determines eligibility of an applicant by examining the value of their assets. In order to become eligible for Medi-Cal the applicant can only have "countable assets" that fall below the **$2,000** limit.

How would that be possible you might ask?

Certain assets are not counted for eligibility purposes if they are determined to be either "exempt" or "unavailable." Some of these assets may come as a surprise. Exempt or unavailable assets for eligibility may include:

- An income producing apartment house;

- Any residence where the applicant claims they have "intent to return home;"

- Both husband's and wife's IRA;

- A building owned with a partner that is unwilling to liquidate is considered "unavailable;"

- A building is "exempt" if it is assessed for tax purposes at a rate lower than the encumbrance on the building, e.g. a building purchased thirty years ago for $50,000 which now has a $500,000 refinance on it;

- Property in litigation is unavailable; and

- Annuities which are irrevocable and immediate are not available during the "string of income."

Property that is not exempt or unavailable must be transferred to somebody else in order not to be counted. That can be a very bad idea. Once that money or property is transferred it is done so irrevocably. The "improvident child" to whom it might be transferred has the right to waste it, sell it, give it away, or just never give it back.

It should be remembered that Medi-Cal is "public assistance." It was not created to assist the rich, nor was it created to assist only the poor. But the world does not rotate around becoming eligible for it. In many cases transferring assets can create far more tax problems for the transferees than is saved by the estate paying for the health care.

Medi-Cal cannot recover its benefits until after both spouses die.

Transferring Your Parent's House To You – A Capital Gains Conundrum.

In the majority of cases where the parent transfers a house to their child during their lifetime it creates a capital gains conundrum. The child receives an immediate benefit upon receiving the house because the state does not reassess the value of the home for tax purposes on a parent-child transfer. (It doesn't reassess on a child-parent transfer either.) Therefore, the child pays no increased property tax.

But, if the child wants to sell the house their parents gifted to them, they are going to be hard hit by long term capital gains.

Suppose your parents bought a three bedroom house in 1956 for $10,000 and it is now worth $880,000. (Those are very realistic numbers in Southern California.) Your parents have been renting the house for the last three years and now decide to gift the house to you.

When they change the title over to you there will be no change in the cost basis of the house. Your parents cost basis "carryovers" to you and therefore you pay no higher property tax on the property than they did. Your cost basis is $10,000.

But what if you want to sell the property? With a cost basis of $10,000, you would pay capital gains tax on an $870,000 gain after a sale for $880,000.

The Federal capital gains tax brackets are complex and shifting, but as of this writing in 2006, the gain on property sold on or after May 6, 2003, is taxed at a rate over 15%.

The California State income tax brackets are the same as the state capital gains brackets. Therefore, a single person with a capital gain of over $40,000, and a married couple with a capital gain of over $80,000 will pay the highest rate of 9.3%.

The math on the property works out as follows:

$880,000 fair market value

$880,000 sale
− $10,000 cost basis

$870,000 gain
− 15%   Fed. tax = $130,000
− 9.3%   State tax = $80,000

You will end up paying $211,000 in taxes.

One alternative to paying these taxes is waiting to inherit the property after your parents die. At that point there will be a "step up" of the cost basis to the fair market value. The cost basis of $10,000 will step up to the sale price of $880,000. (At least, that's the law until the estate tax changes in 2010, after which nobody knows for certain what will happen.)

If you sell your parents' house immediately after death there would be no taxes on the sale if the house did not appreciate in value from the date of death.

This would all seem a little callous if you actually put gift deferment and tax avoidance ahead of the death of your parents. But the beauty of estate planning is to recognize the financial reality of these basic tax consequences and make the best of it – and not be rudely surprised.

For example, according to IRC 121, if a married couple has owned *and* occupied a house for two out of the last five years, they can exclude the first $500,000 of their capital gain from taxes. (It's $250,000 for a single person.)

In the scenario above, your parents could have sold the house they moved from three years ago and paid taxes on only $370,000, reducing the tax bill to $89,910, and saving $121,500 for you.

And if a single homeowner was required to move into a facility due to health reasons they can deduct the first $250,000 of capital gain if they lived in the house one out of five years.

Future Changes For The Inheritance Tax Exemption

As you have seen in the chart under *How The Federal Exemption Tax Works*, the exemption law is scheduled to end after the year 2010. Nobody knows exactly what Congress will do after 2010 and the mystery makes it very difficult to plan.

You cannot plan on what you think Congress *might* do. The talk amongst professionals is that the exemption will come to rest between $2 million and $4 million. Nevertheless, the exemption is presently scheduled to return to $1 million after 2010, although there is even talk of Congress extending the repeal from 2010 to 2016 in order to buy more time.

CONCLUSION

Why You Need An Attorney

You need an attorney for liability reasons. Attorneys are suppose to know what they are doing. If they don't, they risk losing their license or being sued for malpractice. That is strong motivation to do a good job. If an attorney holds him or herself out in the field of estate planning, you can safely assume they can handle your job.

That does not apply to hiring an attorney for litigation. In that case, it doesn't matter if the litigation is over a probate matter or any other kind of court battle, the trial attorney operates on a different field of play.

There are many attorneys whose preference is to never go to court, or to do so only for administrative matters. These are not the persons you want to hire for a Will contest against your brother to get your mother's house back from his manipulative wife. (See *Litigation.*)

But most estate planning issues revolve around a peaceful analysis of what you want to accomplish and how to do it. There is nothing in this guidebook that requires certified specialization for the attorney to apply the general estate planning principals to your life. However, it does mandate that the attorney be knowledgeable on the current state of the law. That is a must.

In large part, that is the purpose of this book. The more familiar you are with the concepts and language of the subject the more accurately you can interface with an attorney to determine if you want to work with them.

Finding The Attorney

There is a general misconception about law firms that must be dispelled.

Many people erroneously believe that to get the best representation you must pay the highest dollar to the largest law firm. Nothing could be further from the truth. Size has nothing to do with quality. The right hand, in many firms, doesn't know what the left hand is doing. You end up paying for their expensive waste and lavish overhead by being charged $2.50 a page for a lousy photocopy.

In this day of modern technology any solo attorney sitting at their desk can have the advantage of a thousand law clerks at their call. What was once the province of the large and prestigious law firm is now at the fingertips of any attorney that subscribes to Lexis or Westlaw, the two largest legal resources in the United States. There is no limitation on an attorney's ability to get answers fast.

Therefore, you can hire any attorney in which you have confidence and not feel guilty that you are settling for something less – as long as he or she is giving you the best deal.

However, many times throughout this guidebook it has been recommended that you seek the advice of a tax expert. In fact, it bears repeating that you will need to seek expert advice from a certified estate planning specialist, tax attorney or CPA any time you are attempting to use complex trusts or business entities to transfer wealth, or to avoid tax consequences, or governmental regulations.

This is particularly true in the areas such as Medi-Cal planning, Special Needs Trust, Family Limited Partnerships, and tax issues for Domestic Partnerships to name a few.

The certified experts are expensive but they are worth it. If they couldn't save people like you lots of money in the long run they wouldn't have a job. There are many, many ways to save money on taxes and savings that are simply beyond the scope of this guidebook.

Scams: A Friendly Warning To The Wise

Beware of Estate Planning tax scams and the con men (or women) selling them. Do not believe a word of something too good to be true.

There is no cutting edge "pure" trust or "Unincorporated Organization" that allows you to not pay taxes. Nor is there some new tax plan so clever that attorneys have not yet heard of them. "No, Virginia, there is no Santa Clause."

The only thing more outrageous than the promises of these estate planning promotions is their appeal to hard working Americans. The con men tell you these are the same closely guarded trusts used by the Rockefellers and the Kennedy Foundation to keep their fortunes in tack for generations. They claim that not only can you pay yourself in dividends which are "never subject to taxes," but your assets held in a PURE TRUST are "beyond the reach of probate and inheritance tax laws."

Don't believe it. There is no such thing. These scams, and what is known as a "Living Trust Mill" where Living Trusts are churned out through seminars using pre-printed forms and no availability to a lawyer, are fairly common.

The illegal ones are sometimes shut down by your local District Attorney and in many cases the scammers are prosecuted and the victims must answer to the IRS.

But these professional cons come back months or years later using different colors, names, faces, brochures, and definitely different catch phrases. "Pure" trust will be changed to "Constitutional" trust, and instead of using the

Rockefellers, they will be friends of the "Alliance for Mature Americans."

For your information, the statute of limitations for the IRS is three years from the date filed or the date due. That three years works both ways: if you made a mistake on your taxes you have three years to amend those tax forms, after which you live with your mistake.

Checking Out The Attorney

You owe it to yourself to make at least an inquiry to your state's Bar Association to make sure the attorney is in good standing and no disciplinary action has been taken against him or her. Remember that anybody can file a complaint, but if there are any complaints that have been filed you need to investigate. If disciplinary action has been taken, find yourself another attorney.

In California the website is Calbar.org.

How To Hire An Attorney

Do not be afraid to pay a *minimum* fee for an initial consultation so you can decide if you like one attorney over the other. Get recommendations from friends and family. Ask your neighbors and associates at clubs and work.

But do not take their word for it. Your friends probably did not read this guidebook and don't know what they are talking about.

Your legacy concerns your most important personal matters; act like it. The best way to approach hiring an attorney is to make two or three different appointments. But before you appear for the consultations have your mind set that you are going to wait and talk to the other attorneys. If one is so good you don't want to wait, then that will be a pleasant surprise and sign the contract. (See *How Much Does It Cost.*) On the other hand, beware of smooth talkers.

Keep this above routine in perspective. If you know all you want is a Living Trust then there is not much to think about. Much has already been said about the nature of the relationship you want with your attorney. Litigation attorneys aside, all the virtues of a Boy Scout are what is best in an attorney...trustworthy, loyal, helpful, friendly, courteous, kind...etc. To that list you want to add extremely knowledgeable and vigilant.

Where do you find such an attorney? Good luck!

YOU SAY GOOD-BYE AND I SAY HELLO

Back in the '60s this Country underwent a cultural revolution in which every Baby Boomer was both a participant and a victim. Whether you were part of the peace movement, the ROTC, Martin Luther King, or the Tin Man, it was an exciting time to be alive. Not everyone was a radical, but it was much like living in the "Roaring Twenties" because life was being explored beyond the limits of all previous conventions. It was *Rebel Without a Cause*, and *2001: A Space Odyssey* all rolled into one huge malaise of a decade or two.

Cultural Revolution was our gift to society. We created the "Pop Culture," but were the last generation to grow up without a personal computer.

The dream of putting a man (golfing?) on the moon was astronomically genius. But not all Baby Boomers share such wonderful memories. In fact, most of us share memories of deep compassion for the death of loved ones. Both Martin Luther King and Robert Kennedy were assassinated within one month of each other in 1968.

There was much anger in society during those days. While hippies freaked out in Golden Gate Park to the virtues of "sex, drugs and rock 'n roll," many of our neighbor's sons were seen being shipped home from "Nam" in a box. It was enough to make every mother cry and every youth frustrated with anger. The question was why nothing was the way our parents said it would be.

We Baby Boomers all lived through those strange days and only we know what they meant to us. But we can all agree on one thing. During the era of Jimi Hendrix, Janis Joplin, and Jim Morrison, (See *Personal Welcome*) "hair" had some aggrandized connotation, some ethereally superior meaning than the cliché of "anti-establishment."

So strong were the feelings against long hair that fathers hated sons for growing it and sons hated fathers for not tolerating it. It was rednecks versus the politically incorrect term of "queer;" it was baby killers versus flag burning cowards, Panthers and Klansmen, and a whole lot of wandering hitchhikers that needed to be stopped – drug dealers and hecklers included. Much blood and violence was shed; and for what? Over hair? Over skin color? Over politics? The Civil Rights Act was only passed in 1964.

Then ten years later every man in America from Alabama to Alaska had long hair of some shape or form. And whether or not it was in or out of style by that time, people had forgotten the reasons for all the social injustices it had created. And guess what? Women stopped wearing bras just for the effect.

Now, entering the year of 2006, two longhaired institutions, Paul McCartney and *The Rolling Stones,* have each finished a combined tour of over 100 American cities, bringing together millions of fans and billions of dollars in concert revenue. In the front rows to the back rows of those sold out stadiums were the doctors, lawyers, teachers, and everyone from the bakers to candlestick-makers that thirty to forty years ago either loved or hated long hair.

What's the point? In defining your legacy try to remember how life's twist and turns affected you. You are your mother and father's child; you are not them. Those family values that seemed so obviously right or wrong back then may not be so for much longer. You need to take the time to reflect on the past to make sure you don't make mistakes in deciding the best way to preserve and distribute your legacy into the future.

Not all longhair stars flamed out like Hendrix, Joplin and Morrison. Others such as McCartney and the *Stones* will be with us forever. The *Stones* played halftime at the Super Bowl for God's sake, 42 years after their first Ed Sullivan show. Did you see Mick Jagger do his same old strut?

We've got a long ways to go. If they can do it, we can do it! But you better believe they have one heck of an estate plan in order.

APPENDIX

Instructions for the Estate Planning Questionnaire

At first blush it may appear the following questionnaire is something more akin to a financial statement than a plan for putting your estate in order. But nothing questioned herein is going to be verified (yet), and secondly the idea is to start thinking about where your money is going to go after you die.

Death is never a happy subject but it's going to happen to all of us. By answering these questions your mind will touch on all the pertinent subjects necessary before putting your last wishes in writing.

It is also the very first piece of evidence showing your state of mind regarding your estate plan, in the event someone would ever make that an issue.

You may feel that many of the questions intrude on your privacy. However, the point is for you to understand the nature of the personal relationship needed with your family and your attorney so you can create the estate plan best suited for you.

Here is the breakdown of data you are asked to provide:

1. Personal identity;
2. Your family (natural objects of your bounty);
3. Your extended family as potential beneficiaries;
4. Potential trustees, guardians and conservators;
5. Assets, both separate and community;
6. Business interest;
7. Potential financial growth;
8. Liabilities;
9. Friends and relatives you trust most; and
10. Financial advisors.

Do the best you can. It's not a test. If nothing else, at least read through the questions and think about your answers.

Mark S. Cornwall
Attorney at Law

EVERYTHING BABY BOOMERS SHOULD KNOW

Estate Planning Questionnaire for Married Clients

1. It is important to know your full names:

   Birth certificate name _____
   _____

   Signature name _____
   _____

   Common name _____
   _____

2. Addresses:

   Residence(s) _____
   _____

   Offices _____
   _____

   Vacation Property _____
   _____

   P.O. Box _____
   _____

3. Home phone, office phone, cell phone, facsimile, email addresses:

    Husband: Best Phone # _____
                   Email _____
                   Others _____

    Wife: Best Phone # _____
                   Email _____
                   Others _____

4. Dates and place of birth:

    Husband _____

    Wife _____

5. Citizenship:

    Husband is a U.S. citizen? _____

    Wife is a U.S. citizen? _____

6. Marital History:

    Date of Marriage: _____

    Place of Marriage: _____

    Date Husband & Wife came to CA if married elsewhere: _____

Children of this marriage (indicate if adopted):

Name   Birth date

_____

_____

_____

_____

7. Husband's prior marriages:

Name of former wife(s) _____

_____

Year of termination of marriages _____

_____

Continuing legal obligations (alimony, child support?) _____

Husband's children of prior Marriages (indicate if adopted):

Name   Birth date
Residence

_____

_____

_____

_____

8. Wife's prior marriages:

Name of former husband(s) _____

_____

Year of termination of marriages _____

_____

Continuing legal obligations (alimony, child support?) _____

Wife's children of prior Marriages (indicate if adopted):

Name   Birth date
Residence

_____

_____

_____

_____

9. Give the name of any adopting parent and which child:_____

_____

10. Deceased children and surviving descendents:

Name   Surviving children

_____

_____

11. Grandchildren:

Name   Parent   Birth date

_____

_____

_____

_____

12. Name of Parents (indicate whether living or deceased):

Husband's parents _____

_____

Wife's parents _____

_____

13. Are there any other relatives whom you are considering as beneficiaries of your estate such as sisters, brothers, nieces nephews?

Name   Age   Relationship

_____

_____

14. Are there any friends or neighbors whom you are considering as beneficiaries of your estate?

   _____

   _____

15. Are there any specific gifts you are both sure you want to gift to specific people?

   _____

   _____

16. Are there any charities you are both sure you want to benefit from your estate?

   _____

   _____

17. Are there any persons named above you would consider for being the trustee of your estate?

   _____

   _____

18. Are there any persons named above you would consider for being the guardian of your children?

   _____

   _____

19. Occupation:
   Husband:

   Name of employer _____

   _____

   Position or occupation _____

   _____

Address _____
_____
Years on this job _____
Telephone _____

Wife:

Name of employer _____
_____
Position or occupation _____
_____
Address _____
_____
Years on this job _____
Telephone _____

20. Social security numbers:

Husband _____
Wife _____

21. Income:

Husband's annual earned income _____
Wife's annual earned income _____
Other community property income _____
Husband's annual separate property
income _____
Wife's annual separate property
income _____

22. Assets:

> This is an important part of your estate planning. A separate worksheet may be necessary. Husband and wife need to agree on what is separate property and what is community property. Much of this is decided by the form of title to the property.

ASSETS

Form of title	Current value
Real Property	_____
Cash & equivalents	_____
Securities	_____
Business interest	_____
Debts receivable	_____
Retirement benefits	_____
Death benefits	_____
Annuities	_____
Life insurance (face value)	_____
Art, jewelry, cars, Furniture, etc.	_____
	_____
Other assets	_____
	_____

What was your approximate net worth the day before you were married?

Husband _____   Wife _____

Which of your holdings or assets do you believe have the most potential for significant appreciation over the years?

_____

Do you anticipate obtaining assets of significant value over the next few years? If so, what is the plan?

_____

If you own a business or partnership in a business please explain your ownership interest and its value.

_____

_____

23. Major liabilities:

　　　　Mortgages:

　　　　　　1._____

　　　　　　_____

　　　　　　2._____

　　　　　　_____

　　　　　　3._____

　　　　　　_____

Commercial loans:

1._____

_____

2._____

_____

3._____

_____

Debts to private parties:

1._____

_____

2._____

_____

3._____

_____

Other debts (please describe):

1._____

_____

2._____

_____

3._____

_____

24. Have you guaranteed any loans?

Primary obligor   Amount guaranteed

_____

_____

_____

_____

25. Questions that affect the outcome of your estate:

> Have you read *Everything A Baby Boomer Should Know (Before Talking To An Attorney)?*   Yes _____ No _____
>
> Have you entered into any prenuptial agreements or transmutation agreements affecting the ownership of your property? Yes _____ No _____
>
> Have you made any gifts over $10,000 after 1981? Yes _____ No _____
>
> Have you created any trust? Yes _____ No _____
>
> Have you received any substantial inheritance? Yes _____ No _____

Do you expect to receive any substantial inheritance?
Yes _____ No _____

Are you the beneficiary of any trust?
Yes _____ No _____

Are there persons whom you may want to disinherit?
Yes _____ No _____

Are there any persons who have special needs you would like to provide for?
Yes _____ No _____

26. Please list your current advisors:

Accountant:_____
_____

Financial advisor:_____
_____

Life Insurance agent:_____
_____

Securities broker:_____
_____

Investment advisor:_____
_____

Your most trusted friend:

    Wife:_____

    Husband:_____

Your most trusted relative:

    Wife:_____

    Husband:_____

27. Who is your first choice to be the conservator over your estate after your husband or wife is gone?

    Wife's first choice _____

    Husband's first choice _____

    Wife's second choice _____

    Husband's second choice _____

PROFILE

Mark S. Cornwall
Attorney at Law

"Where I live in Alexandria, Virginia, near the Supreme Court building there is a toll bridge across the Potomac River. When in a rush, I pay the toll and get home early. However, I usually drive outside the downtown section of the city, and cross the Potomac on a free bridge. If I went over the toll bridge and through the toll without paying I would be guilty of tax evasion. However, if I go the extra mile and drive outside the city of Washington to the free bridge, I am using a legitimate, logical and suitable method of tax avoidance. And, I am providing a useful social service as well."

(Louis D. Brandeis, U.S. Supreme Court Justice)

For twenty years I was a trial attorney. For twenty years I stood before judges and juries and argued the merits of my clients' cases. Sometimes, in the heat of the stuffy courtroom, I would sweat blood over the judge's rulings or a witness's statement on cross-examination. But one thing that never changed was the clenching in my stomach every time I watched a jury walk back into the jury box with their verdict, and I attempted to read their faces.

180

I was never able to read their faces – win or lose. It always seemed the one person that nodded their head up and down in agreement with everything I said turned out to be the one juror that voted against me.

It is a crazy business. If I lost, sometimes I would appeal and my appellate victories have been published in both Federal and California State Appellate courts. If I won, my opponent would appeal and sometimes my victories would be sent back to the trial court on remittitur for a new trial.

Millions of dollars in settlements and jury verdicts later, it still seemed that nobody was ever happy with the outcome. There were probably five clients during that period of my career that actually understood and appreciated the magnificent job that had been accomplished by so many people working so hard on their behalf.

That's why I jumped from that stressful warship and dove swimmingly into the peaceful waters of estate planning. I wanted to provide a service that would produce an identifiable product and give immediate gratification to my clients. There is no better peace of mind than knowing your home is in order, your loved ones are cared for, and you have done your job.

The Goal Of This Guidebook: Empowerment

How can a Baby Boomer possibly plan their estate if they don't know anything about it? If they thought all they needed was a Living Trust they may be surprised to know a married couple needs not only a Living Trust, and two Pourover Wills, but perhaps a transmutation agreement for the best tax benefits, or at least a property agreement, and certainly a transfer of title to personal property into the trust.

The goal of this guidebook is to give everyone that reads it the ability to know what they are talking about. You must have some idea of where you want to go and what you want to do there. You are an intelligent person and this guidebook will give you everything you need to know to protect your family and make you a hero.

ACKNOWLEDGMENTS

The author would like to acknowledge all of the attorneys of National and California acclaim whose legal treatises and other scholarly writings and reviews, have contributed to this book. These experts' public and private opinions regarding very complicated issues, and their creative and humorous teachings on the subject of estate planning have made this book possible.

More specifically the author would like to thank all contributors to the Continuing Education Of The California Bar for their efforts to provide the most intelligent and comprehensive educational information available to the general public through the education of the members of the bar.

BONANZA

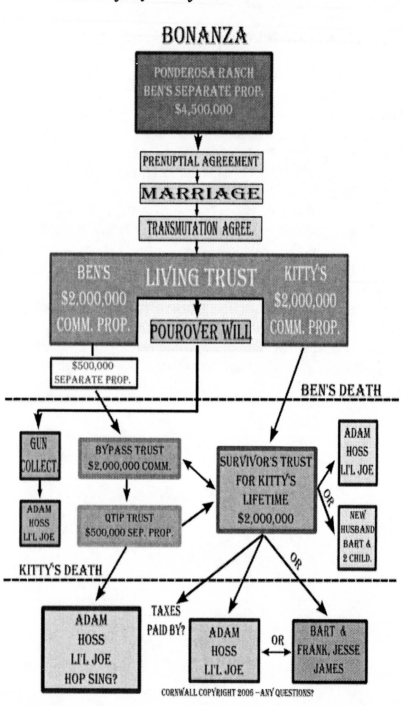

PONDEROSA RANCH
BEN'S SEPARATE PROP.
$4,500,000

PRENUPTIAL AGREEMENT

MARRIAGE

TRANSMUTATION AGREE.

BEN'S
$2,000,000
COMM. PROP.

LIVING TRUST

KITTY'S
$2,000,000
COMM. PROP.

POUROVER WILL

$500,000
SEPARATE PROP.

BEN'S DEATH

GUN
COLLECT.

BYPASS TRUST
$2,000,000 COMM.

SURVIVOR'S TRUST
FOR KITTY'S
LIFETIME
$2,000,000

ADAM
HOSS
LI'L JOE

ADAM
HOSS
LI'L JOE

QTIP TRUST
$500,000 SEP. PROP.

OR

NEW
HUSBAND
BART &
2 CHILD.

KITTY'S DEATH

OR

ADAM
HOSS
LI'L JOE
HOP SING?

TAXES
PAID BY?

ADAM
HOSS
LI'L JOE

OR

BART &
FRANK, JESSE
JAMES

CORNWALL COPYRIGHT 2006 --ANY QUESTIONS?

184

BONANZA -- TRADITIONAL

PONDEROSA RANCH
BEN'S SEPARATE PROP.
$4,500,000

MARRIAGE

BEN'S $2,000,000 COMM. PROP.　LIVING TRUST　KITTY'S $2,000,000 COMM. PROP.

POUROVER WILL

$500,000 SEPARATE PROP.

BEN'S DEATH

GUN COLLECT

BYPASS TRUST $2,000,000 COMM.

SURVIVOR'S TRUST FOR KITTY'S LIFETIME $2,000,000

ADAM HOSS LI'L JOE

QTIP TRUST $500,000 SEP. PROP.

KITTY'S DEATH

ADAM HOSS LI'L JOE HOP SING?

ADAM HOSS LI'L JOE

CORNWALL COPYRIGHT 2006 --ANY QUESTIONS?

BONANZA -- REMARRIED

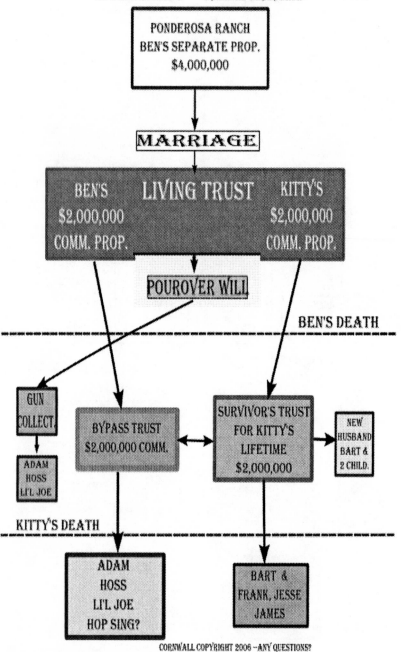

PONDEROSA RANCH
BEN'S SEPARATE PROP.
$4,000,000

MARRIAGE

BEN'S $2,000,000 COMM. PROP.
LIVING TRUST
KITTY'S $2,000,000 COMM. PROP.

POUROVER WILL

BEN'S DEATH

GUN COLLECT

ADAM HOSS LI'L JOE

BYPASS TRUST $2,000,000 COMM.

SURVIVOR'S TRUST FOR KITTY'S LIFETIME $2,000,000

NEW HUSBAND BART & 2 CHILD.

KITTY'S DEATH

ADAM HOSS LI'L JOE HOP SING?

BART & FRANK, JESSE JAMES

CORNWALL COPYRIGHT 2006 --ANY QUESTIONS?

DR. DENTIST AND NORA

LIVING TRUST

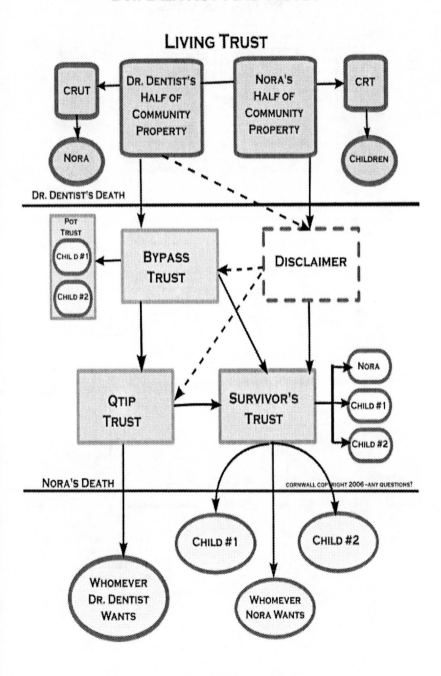

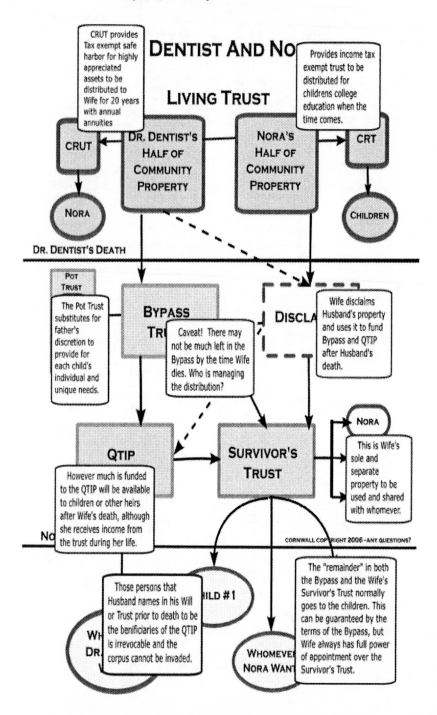

DENTIST AND NO...

LIVING TRUST

CRUT provides Tax exempt safe harbor for highly appreciated assets to be distributed to Wife for 20 years with annual annuities

Provides income tax exempt trust to be distributed for childrens college education when the time comes.

CRUT

DR. DENTIST'S HALF OF COMMUNITY PROPERTY

NORA'S HALF OF COMMUNITY PROPERTY

CRT

NORA

CHILDREN

DR. DENTIST'S DEATH

POT TRUST

The Pot Trust substitutes for father's discretion to provide for each child's individual and unique needs.

BYPASS TR...

Caveat! There may not be much left in the Bypass by the time Wife dies. Who is managing the distribution?

DISCLA...

Wife disclaims Husband's property and uses it to fund Bypass and QTIP after Husband's death.

QTIP

However much is funded to the QTIP will be available to children or other heirs after Wife's death, although she receives income from the trust during her life.

SURVIVOR'S TRUST

NORA

This is Wife's sole and separate property to be used and shared with whomever.

No...

CORNWALL COPYRIGHT 2006 –ANY QUESTIONS?

Those persons that Husband names in his Will or Trust prior to death to be the benificiaries of the QTIP is irrevocable and the corpus cannot be invaded.

...ILD #1

WH... DR...

WHOMEVE... NORA WAN...

The "remainder" in both the Bypass and the Wife's Survivor's Trust normally goes to the children. This can be guaranteed by the terms of the Bypass, but Wife always has full power of appointment over the Survivor's Trust.

WALT THE PLUMBING CONTRACTOR

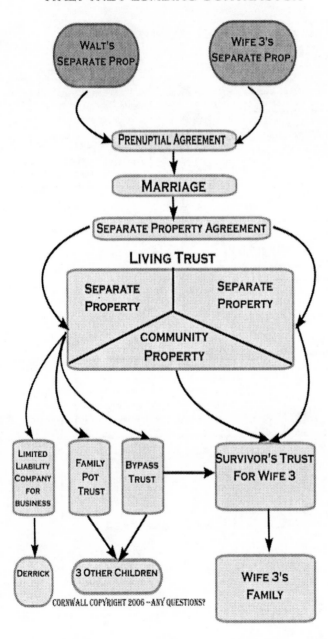

CORNWALL COPYRIGHT 2006 -- ANY QUESTIONS?

WALT THE PLUMBING CONTRACTOR

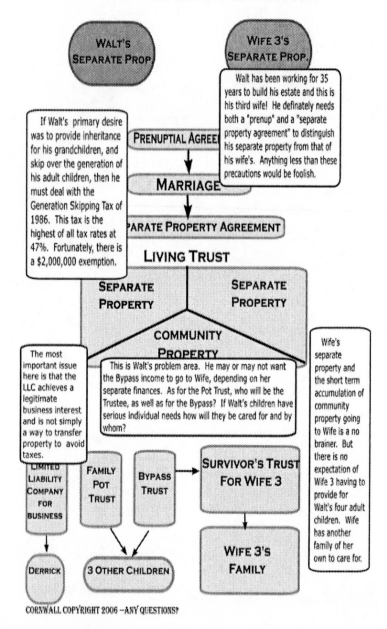

WALT'S SEPARATE PROP

WIFE 3'S SEPARATE PROP.

Walt has been working for 35 years to build his estate and this is his third wife! He definately needs both a "prenup" and a "separate property agreement" to distinguish his separate property from that of his wife's. Anything less than these precautions would be foolish.

If Walt's primary desire was to provide inheritance for his grandchildren, and skip over the generation of his adult children, then he must deal with the Generation Skipping Tax of 1986. This tax is the highest of all tax rates at 47%. Fortunately, there is a $2,000,000 exemption.

PRENUPTIAL AGREE

MARRIAGE

PARATE PROPERTY AGREEMENT

LIVING TRUST

SEPARATE PROPERTY

SEPARATE PROPERTY

COMMUNITY PROPERTY

The most important issue here is that the LLC achieves a legitimate business interest and is not simply a way to transfer property to avoid taxes.

This is Walt's problem area. He may or may not want the Bypass income to go to Wife, depending on her separate finances. As for the Pot Trust, who will be the Trustee, as well as for the Bypass? If Walt's children have serious individual needs how will they be cared for and by whom?

Wife's separate property and the short term accumulation of community property going to Wife is a no brainer. But there is no expectation of Wife 3 having to provide for Walt's four adult children. Wife has another family of her own to care for.

LIMITED LIABILITY COMPANY FOR BUSINESS

FAMILY POT TRUST

BYPASS TRUST

SURVIVOR'S TRUST FOR WIFE 3

DERRICK

3 OTHER CHILDREN

WIFE 3'S FAMILY

INDEX

Printed in the United States
58678LVS00004B/111